AGILE UX STORYTELLING

CRAFTING STORIES FOR BETTER SOFTWARE DEVELOPMENT

Rebecca Baker

ca ®

technologies

CA Press

Apress®

Agile UX Storytelling: Crafting Stories for Better Software Development

Rebecca Baker
Plano, Texas, USA

ISBN-13 (pbk): 978-1-4842-2996-5
DOI 10.1007/978-1-4842-2997-2

ISBN-13 (electronic): 978-1-4842-2997-2

Library of Congress Control Number: 2017952245

Managing Director: Welmoed Spahr
Editorial Director: Todd Green
Acquisitions Editor: Susan McDermott
Development Editor: Laura Berendson
Technical Reviewer: Ben Doctor
Illustrator: Arielle McMahon
Coordinating Editor: Rita Fernando
Copy Editor: Kim Wimpsett
Cover: eStudio Calamar

Distributed to the book trade worldwide by Springer Science+Business Media New York, 233 Spring Street, 6th Floor, New York, NY 10013. Phone 1-800-SPRINGER, fax (201) 348-4505, e-mail orders-ny@springer-sbm.com, or visit www.springeronline.com. Apress Media, LLC is a California LLC and the sole member (owner) is Springer Science + Business Media Finance Inc (SSBM Finance Inc). SSBM Finance Inc is a **Delaware** corporation.

For information on translations, please e-mail rights@apress.com, or visit www.apress.com/rights-permissions.

Apress titles may be purchased in bulk for academic, corporate, or promotional use. eBook versions and licenses are also available for most titles. For more information, reference our Print and eBook Bulk Sales web page at www.apress.com/bulk-sales.

Any source code or other supplementary material referenced by the author in this book is available to readers on GitHub via the book's product page, located at www.apress.com/9781484229965. For more detailed information, please visit www.apress.com/source-code.

This book is dedicated to all those bought this book because it had the words zombie and software on the cover. You are my kind of people.

Contents

About the Author vii

About the Technical Reviewer ix

About the Illustrator xi

Acknowledgments xiii

Preface: Not Just Once Upon a Time xv

Chapter 1: A New Project 1

Chapter 2: The Storyteller 7

Chapter 3: The Plan 17

Chapter 4: A Visit 25

Chapter 5: Field Work 35

Chapter 6: The Horror Stories 43

Chapter 7: The Wreckage 51

Chapter 8: The Balance 57

Chapter 9: Problems 65

Chapter 10: Personas and Journey Maps 75

Chapter 11: Sharing the Research 81

Chapter 12: Architecture 91

Chapter 13: Problem-Solving 107

Chapter 14: Revelations 117

Chapter 15: MVP 127

Chapter 16: The Bid 133

Chapter 17: Epilogue: Finding a Happily Ever After 137

About the Author

Dr. Rebecca Baker is a professional speaker and passionate storyteller with more than 20 publications and 30 speaking engagements on topics ranging from information encapsulation to remote usability testing. A patent holder with 20+ years of enterprise software experience, Rebecca is currently the senior director of user interaction design and research at Active Network, where she instituted a story-based design approach to feature planning and development. She was formerly the UX design director and product design manager at CA Technologies. Rebecca received her BS in physics from the University of Houston and her PhD in Information Science from the University of North Texas. As a writer of both fiction and nonfiction, she believes that storytelling should not be relegated to fairy tales but can work to make information more accessible, understandable, memorable, and actionable in everyday work.

About the Technical Reviewer

Ben Doctor is the global experience research manager at Active Network, a Vista Equity Partners portfolio company. His group spans market and HCI research and is tightly coupled with IxD, VisD, engineering, and product management. Ben has written and spoken on design process, applied research methods, prototyping, and product innovation.

Ben earned an MBA from the Rady School of Management at UC San Diego and a BSc from UC Santa Barbara.

About the Illustrator

Arielle McMahon is a product designer and freelance illustrator based in Dallas, Texas. Arielle attended Texas A&M University – Commerce where she received a BFA in visual communications. She enjoys print design, long walks on the beach, and puppies.

Arielle can be reached at ajademcmahon@gmail.com.

Acknowledgments

I would like to express my gratitude to the following individuals who made this book possible:

Editors, illustrator, advisors: Ben Doctor for his brutally honest and insightful comments that prevented the zombies from taking over this book and instead made it useful. Rita Fernando, Robert Hutchinson, Susan McDermott, and Laura Berendson for their patience, encouragement, patience, keen direction, and did I mention patience as we traveled this path together. Arielle McMahon for her wonderful, playful illustrations that add so much to the book. And Karen Sleeth for inspiring me to be crazy enough to write a software book with zombies in it.

Family: My husband, John Baker, for his love, his tireless support of this pursuit, and his willingness to keep the kids out my hair while I wrote. My parents, Larry and Sally, for instilling in me the belief that I can do anything I set my mind to and providing the tools to make that possible. And my children, John, Zoe, and William, for telling all their friends that their mom is a writer.

Friends: Russ Wilson and Jeff Noble, who introduced me to Apress and cheered me on. And Ambra Tieszen who promised to "read the shit out of it" if I could finish this book. I'm holding you to that.

And God, for blessing me with the opportunity to write this book and the stubbornness to complete it.

Preface: Not Just Once Upon a Time

Understanding the Relevance of Stories

When I was a child, I loved stories. I loved to hear them, I loved to tell them, I loved to write them. It seemed to me that the whole world was filled with stories, if you were only willing to listen. Whether it is the charming elderly man on the train telling me how he used to dance in thunderstorms without fear because lightening is nothing but the shoes of the angels striking the clouds as they dance, the proud crowing of a parent in the grocery store whose child just took first place in her chess tournament, or the product manager relaying how he sees a certain friend once a year to watch him run a marathon and how that experience inspired him to create an app for spectators—I love stories because they give you a version of the world as seen through someone else's eyes.

As I grew up and began working in enterprise software, I realized, as many others have, stories are not just for children. They are powerful, relevant tools that can be used every day to ensure effective and accurate communication, to persuade others by helping them see your point of view, and to improve your products by giving the faceless "user" who buys your software a face. At all parts of the software development life cycle, you can find people using stories—not just the traditional user story associated with the Agile methodology but narratives of every kind that illustrate ideas and concepts in a way that people can understand. Product management uses stories to communicate their business cases, helping others understand the problem they are trying to solve. Business analysts use stories to tease out detailed requirements. Designers use stories to humanize and personalize the end user to prioritize pain points and find the best solution. Developers use stories to provide context and priority to coding decisions. Quality assurance people use stories to create realistic test scenarios. Support people use stories to communicate solutions to end users. These stories show a vision of things from a different angle. And in that vision lives perspective, context, and understanding.

What Is a Story?

On its surface, a story is a narrative that describes a series of events—an accounting of something either fictional or nonfictional. However, ask any child, and they will be quick to tell you that a list of what happened—whether real or imagined—is *not* a story. So, what then differentiates the simple recounting of events from a tale worth telling? The secret to stories is meaning.[1] When we tell a story, we give the events we are recounting meaning through the details we provide, the details we leave out, the tone, the context, the characters, and the conclusion. We provide our listener or reader not just a series of facts but our interpretation of those facts.

Stories can be made of words, images, or sounds. A short film clip showing current conditions in a war-torn country, a well-drawn political cartoon, the recounting of a site visit by a product manager, the headliner in a newspaper—all of these are stories. Regardless of the format used, they convey the storyteller's perspective of an event or situation, their reaction to it, and the filter they use to understand it.

---

[1] Phillip Martin, *How to Write Your Best Story: Advice for Writers On Spinning an Enchanting Tale* (Milwaukee, WI: Crickhollow Books, 2011).

The Power of Stories

The power of stories lies not in the entertainment they may provide but in the glimpse into another person's mind and vision, as a participant rather than an observer. Stories show you how other people see the world and those things that happen within that world. They let us see how another person's interpretation of events is different from our own and how it is the same. They let us cheat Schrodinger's cat[2] and observe it simultaneously alive and dead. And once we have that perspective, they give us the power to show others how we see the world.

Persuade

One of the most common uses for stories is to persuade. Think about the commercials you see every day, whether on the television, on the radio, in magazines, or on the Internet. A good commercial tells a story to persuade you to see things from the advertiser's point of view. One story might show a young woman out on a date with a young man in a fancy sports car. What story does this scene imply about the role of the car for this young man? Another shows a happy family seated around a table, laughing and conversing, about to eat a prepackaged convenience food that looks tantalizingly delicious. By showing us a story of a happy family who eats together, what is the advertiser persuading us to believe? Stories have the power to associate powerful imagery with strong emotions, leading the audience to conclusions they might not have drawn otherwise.[3]

Context helps others understand our perspective and personalizes data, making it easier to get key ideas across. A design team that I led was having a challenging time explaining the reason to a client we were making some improvements to some software that let a user plan a trip. The team was getting frustrated—they had shown the numbers, time on task, and so on, but the client just wasn't getting it. Taking a step back, to walk them through the full set of changes, we created a story about a young woman who wanted

---

[2]Schrodinger's cat refers to a famous thought experiment by the physicist Erwin Schrodinger in the 1930s. In it, a cat is placed in a box along with a jar of poison and a radioactive isotope. If the isotope decays, the jar breaks, and the cat dies. However, since the box is sealed, there is no way of telling whether this has happened or not without opening the box and looking at the cat. While the box is closed, the cat is considered simultaneously dead and alive. The act of opening the box and observing the cat forces the system to be one or the other. This illustrates the idea of quantum superposition and how reality forces a single state on a system. Put another way, it shows that once we observe something, it is forever changed from multiple potentials to a single reality.
[3]John Baldoni, "Using Stories to Persuade," *Harvard Business Review*, March 24, 2011, https://hbr.org/2011/03/using-stories-as-a-tool-of-per.

to take a trip. We explained how excited the young woman was to go on the trip but that she was anxious too because she'd never done anything like this before. At each step of her journey, we told her story and how our designs had helped her, keeping her feeling connected and calm. After the presentation, the client came to me to say, "You guys really get it—this is how our customers live!" They approved the changes the same day, and we were able to move forward. The challenge had been that they couldn't "see" the numbers. They weren't real; they weren't the people they dealt with on a daily basis. It took creating story to explain a vision that we could share with them to help persuade them to see our perspective and, more importantly, their user's perspective.

Using stories to persuade is a powerful technique and, as such, imposes an ethical responsibility on the storyteller. Stories must be based on real data—not simply made up to support the beliefs of the storyteller. Inspiring stories can lead us to invest in a particular opportunity or change our health habits, which can be dangerous to our finances and health if they are not adequately fact-based.[4]

Educate

Stories make things more memorable. Whether used as a coaching tool or a way to help people understand a new concept or process, stories make things relatable. As pattern-seeking creatures, we are wired to look for stories.[5] By providing the story for our audience, we give them context to make sense of what we are trying to communicate.

To teach some designers about the context of the software they were designing, I used this story to illustrate how the software would help check in children to a daycare center:

> The day started like any other, with Miss Mary Martinez checking in children at KidSpot. There were so many things planned for the day—making paper flowers, feeding the goldfish, learning how to count to five, and let's not forget Jillian Gorfman's birthday cupcakes that afternoon—that Miss Mary was not quite paying attention to all the little heads coming through her

[4]David Evans, "Danger of Stories," December 18, 2003, http://blogs.worldbank.org/publicsphere/danger-stories.
[5]Melanie C. Green, "Storytelling in Teaching," *Association for Psychological Science*, April 1, 2004, www.psychologicalscience.org/observer/storytelling-in-teaching#.WR4EzFYrLmE.

door. At the end of the day, she prepared for the parents to come pick up their sticky little darlings, wiping cupcake icing from their ears and reassuring them that it would be their turn any moment. But wait! She counted the ears she had wiped and came up with two too few! Quickly checking her roster, she noticed that in her hurry this morning she had failed to check every child in. She quickly checks in the ones she can see, but Sue Ellen Dempsie is nowhere to be found. Did she make it in this morning? Miss Mary can't remember, and unfortunately Sue Ellen is a "hider." She starts to sweat, checking every possible hiding place Sue Ellen might be.

Once the designers had internalized the story, I started asking questions. What do we know about the environment that the check-in software is used in? What level of care and attention is the teacher able to give the software? What does this tell you about the design? The students were able to quickly hone in on the need for a simple interface with potentially a fail-safe check-in feature requiring a physical interaction with the child (swipe a badge or a quick photo of the child), a dual check-in (once at the facility level and once at the class level), and an alert that let the teacher know if all the expected children had not checked in. The original designs for the class exercise that had concentrated on extensive reporting that would run overnight, options for assigning nicknames, and so on, were adjusted based on a more visceral understanding of the situation faced by the teachers.

Communicate

Every person has their own set of stories. They collect them from the time they are born, adding their own narratives about their personal experiences as well as the narratives of their peers, their mentors, and their society. These stories inform how they understand the world—they are the filter through which they see things. Understanding these stories can make or break the communication between two people. On a cultural level,[6] stories can inform an entire society's attitude toward impactful things such as expected behaviors and outcomes, organizational responsibilities and authority, and acceptable uncertainties.

When working with designers in China, I have been asked, "How can I better understand the end users when they are Americans?" YouTube is a

---

[6]Geert Hofstede, Gert Jan Hofstede, and Michael Minkov, *Cultures and Organizations: Software of the Mind*, 3rd ed. (New York: McGraw-Hill, 2010).

great resource for this, as you can find endless videos people have made of themselves telling their stories. However, for a deeper understanding of cultural differences, I frequently point to fairy tales. Many children's stories and fairy tales represent the cultural lessons we want our children to learn.[7] Take the classic tale of Cinderella—hard work and endurance in the face of abuse will eventually pay off royally! Good triumphs over evil. Contrast this with classic Chinese folk tales, and you will see a very different message—one of balance, of the need for both good and evil. As I pointed this out to the team, one of the designers suddenly had an "aha!" look on her face. When I asked her about it, she said she realized now why her North American colleagues always celebrated when they hit a milestone. She said, "It's like they didn't even know that this was just temporary and that something else would come up to push us down again in the cycle." The difference in approach is part of our cultural story.

A Story of Stories

This book is a story of stories. Through the fictional story of Max, you will see how stories can be used in software development to maintain context, discover issues (before they blow up—literally or figuratively), and solve problems. Each chapter will tell you a bit more about stories and help you see, through the character's perspective, how you might be able to use stories yourself. Even if you don't have to deal with zombies.

Key Takeaways

- Stories provide power when communicating by providing a visceral, human connection to numbers and facts.

- Stories can be used to persuade, communicate, and relate, providing a glimpse of a different perspective.

- Good software design must be thoughtful and inclusive of the end user. Using stories, everyone in the process from product manager to BA to designer to developer to QA to support can transform data into something with meaning.

---

[7]Jack Zipes, *The Irresistible Fairy Tale: The Cultural and Social History of a Genre* (Princeton, 2012).

A New Project

The dusty green sedan in front of him stopped abruptly, causing Max to swear loudly and slam on the brakes. His black compact SUV complied, rocking forward with the sudden absence of momentum. Wincing, he heard his backpack, lunch, range bag, and all the junk he kept saying he was going to clear out of the trunk slide forward in a tumbling crash. *That's going to be a mess*, he thought. Glancing up the road, he could see only a few cars stopped. A figure wound through them, seemingly lost, stopping to try to get into each car, pounding on the window. *Great—a deader.*

As if on cue, his phone rang. He flicked on the speaker phone, keeping his eyes on the wandering menace in the road.

"What's the password?" he asked.

"Max is an asshole," came the quick reply.

"Love you too, man. Look, I'm stuck in traffic on 635. It's going to have to wait, whatever it is."

"Tell that to the boss! She's got that crazy smile that says 'money' and 'insane deadlines' and is bugging me every five minutes to see if you're here yet."

"Well, tell her to beam me up, because it's a deader gridlock. No telling how long it will take to clear it off the road."

Max jumped as a fist slammed against the SUV. Male, late 40s, clothes dirty but not yet ragged. Newly infected. You only ever saw the new ones these days. But that was enough. Its eyes were wild, rolling to fix on Max as it tried to work the door handle, pounding on the zombie-proof glass.

© Rebecca Baker and CA 2017

R. Baker, *Agile UX Storytelling*, DOI 10.1007/978-1-4842-2997-2_1

Breathing hard, Max tried to get his heartbeat under control while ignoring the *thing*. It moaned, scratching at the glass. The law said he had to sit tight and wait for the authorities, but his finger itched to grab his Glock and take care of this vermin right now. Of course, his Glock was in the back, probably buried under his PB&J and gym socks. If there hadn't been so many mistakes made by over-enthusiastic shooters…but there had been, and now he had to sit here and wait.

"Yo! You still there, Max?" The phone squawked at him, bringing him back to the conversation.

"Yeah, yeah, still here. What's Angie want anyway?" He pictured the CEO of Where's The Zombie, blonde hair pulled back in a haphazard ponytail, Cheshire cat grin on her face.

"We just bought Virtual Undead. The announcement goes out in an hour."

Max nearly choked. "The movement simulation software? What on Earth for?"

"Something about integrating it with our stuff for an RFP?[1] I dunno—I just work here, dude."

"Hey, you're the product manager! You've got to ask these questions!"

"What, you think I didn't ask? She said I had to wait until the oh-holy designer Max the Magnificent got in before she would deign to answer any questions. So, get your ass in here so I can find out what we're trying to do."

Max sighed. He'd been working at Where's The Zombie for a year now, designing the entire interface for its zombie-tracking software. They'd only just gotten a user researcher and visual designer in the month previous, and it had been a huge relief not to have to be a one-man shop anymore. Now this—integrating an entire simulation package? Angie had lost it this time. He quickly thought through what he'd have to tell his new team. Sylvia, the new user researcher, was going to freak for sure. She was already pissed about the lack of background research they had on people using their software and short deadlines that precluded usability testing. This sounded like it was going to be a total fire-drill approach. They'd be lucky if they had time to even spell *persona* let alone create them.

"Do Sylvia and Geoffrey know yet?"

"Sylvia does—you know she gets here at 7 a.m.? What kind of crazy person goes to work at 7 a.m.? That's just messed up. Geoffrey's not in yet."

---

[1] RFP: Request for Proposal. A solicitation for bids for a product or service that outlines the requirements and needs of the company/government/agency requesting the bids.

He could see the blue lights of the deader squad approaching the wrong way down the highway. About time they showed up, he thought. The zombie at his window looked up, spotting the lights. It straightened, staring first up the highway and then down at Max, much to his surprise. That was not possible, he thought. Zombies didn't "look" at you or at anything—they just shuffled slowly and menacingly toward the nearest human and…Max cut off the thought before his brain could start providing the gruesome pictures. Then the zombie turned and did the impossible—it sprinted (sprinted?!) into the brush at the side of the highway.

"Uh, Justin…," Max stared open-mouthed after the rapidly disappearing zombie as it ducked around a tree and headed into a neighborhood. "I think our movement algorithms are going to need a serious adjustment."

"What? Wait, I don't want to know. Just get in here fast. I've got a war room set up."

"Have they got a design team?"

"Yeah, yeah, they do—couple of hotshots out of Austin and someone they call the 'storyteller,' whatever the hell that is. Listen—I need to get going. Get your game face on."

"Sure thing." Max hung up, watching as the deader squad in tactical gear worked through the cars, pulse rifles slung low. They skimmed past his SUV, automatically checking under his car and looking in the back windows. As they moved on, the traffic started moving again albeit slowly. Max shifted back into gear and eased forward, eyes drawn to the neighborhood the zombie had run. (Had he really seen it run? How could that be possible?) As he looked, he saw several people in hazmat suits appear from behind a pickup truck. What the…? Max squinted—they had some kind of electronic equipment with them that they kept checking.

A loud honk brought his attention back to the road, which was now clear in front of him. A quick glance back, and they were gone. He accelerated forward, turning toward the office.

Storyteller? He smiled slightly imagining the movie *The Princess Bride* and the old man telling his grandson "As you wish." Probably not anything that entertaining. However, Max had been reading a lot about stories lately—where was that? One of the industry blogs? He couldn't remember. He was intrigued in spite of himself. He always loved a good story, even if it was just Sylvia telling him about a site visit. It helped him envision what it was like to use his designs. He took the exit ramp for downtown, winding through the deserted streets. No one walked outside anymore—not in open areas. The possibility of being attacked, albeit small these days, was still too real for people to risk it. He turned toward the parking box building. Once a traditional parking garage, it had been converted to provide a secure way for people to move from their cars to the buildings. The entrance was a solid steel box about the size of a large SUV, open to the street. Once inside, a door would slide shut behind the vehicle, enclosing the car. Scanners would run the length of the box, checking for deaders. If none was found, the whole assembly would move to the first open floor, like a giant elevator, and you could drive out and park. If you weren't clear...Max shuddered thinking of how he'd heard the alarms go off last month. Carefully pulling in, he put the car in park and turned off the ignition. The large metal door slid closed behind him with an ominous clang. Max understood the precaution, but he always felt a little claustrophobic while he waited for the scanners to confirm his car was zombie-free. The metal box hummed with sound waves crafted to detect the peculiar electromagnetic resonance found in deaders. It made his nose itch. The light in the box moved from red to green, and he felt the drop in his stomach as the box moved abruptly upward three stories. The door slid open, and he started the car back up, rolling forward into the garage.

It had been ten years since the first zombie shambled out of a university lab and started biting students. No one knew it was a problem at first. Just some kids and a bad flu—a flu that made people slow, shambling figures who couldn't talk or recognize their families and who would try to bite anyone not infected. Then those who got bitten started to get sick, and no one got better. There had been widespread panic—people barricading themselves indoors, waiting for the ravening hordes to overcome them. The government stepped in, quarantining whole communities. Still, some of the deaders got through, and the spread continued. But it was a slow spread, and the world quickly learned that some basic precautions allowed life to continue almost like it had before. For the most part, zombies were plagued with the same issues as their live counterparts—unlike the movies, they were averse to getting hurt and could be disabled and killed like normal humans. Soon, a whole industry opened up with anti-zombie measures, both offensive and defensive. Where's The Zombie had sprung up like so many other software groups to take advantage of people's new need for information on zombie locations. Using sophisticated satellite networks combined with drones, Where's The Zombie was able to detect and confirm zombie risings and movements. Other companies modeled their movements to make targeting more effective. Scanners, security systems, transportation improvements, and more—the tech industry rose to meet the new threat eagerly. Through the miracle of technology, a new "normal" had been achieved. But, despite amazing advances and aggressive government countermeasures, the zombie problem persisted. Outside of conspiracy theorists, no one seemed to know why. Uprisings continued with alarming frequency, with no discernible pattern. It was not a relaxed kind of world to live in.

After parking, Max stepped out of his car, automatically hitting the lift button for the back hatch.

"Argh!" He had forgotten about the sudden stop back on 635. All his belongings lay in a heap against the back seat. Grumbling, he bent to pick through the detritus, digging through discarded fast-food bags and water bottles, and made a silent promise that tonight he would clean it out. Really. He stuffed his lunch into his backpack along with some sketches that had slid out. He had been working on some new concepts for the primary screen—currently his emphasis on display had been geographically centered on the subject's current location. Based on feedback that Sylvia had gathered, Max saw an opportunity for changing the static, current location display to a route-based, predictive display, like a weather map but with zombie uprisings. He sighed as he glanced at them. That project would need to wait now.

Grabbing his backpack and closing the trunk, he slung it over one shoulder and turned to make his way into the office. A quick glimpse in the side mirror made him wince. If he'd known he was meeting a new company today…his "Team Browncoats" T-shirt and semi-clean jeans were not likely to make a great impression. On the other hand, he didn't have some goofy title like "storyteller." He grinned at that and headed in.

Key Takeaways

- Setting the scene is key in creating effective stories. You must provide background and context to help people understand the circumstances in which your characters find themselves—which makes them relatable.

- Include elements in your setting that are relevant, but nothing else. In this setting, it is important to understand how the world has changed, how zombies act, and what Max was working on prior to this new, unexpected project. It is not important to know how many siblings Max might have, whether he likes cats, or what his degree is in. At best, irrelevant details distract the audience from the point of your story and, at worst, may lead them to a false conclusion.

The Storyteller

The office seemed unusually empty as Max walked in. He found his way to the main conference room, opening the door to a cacophony of excited voices.

"Max! You're here! Great! Grab a bagel, and let's get started."

Angie looked like she might spontaneously combust at any minute. He'd seen her excited before, but this was ridiculous—eyes darting constantly around the room, clicking her favorite gel pen repeatedly, pacing back and forth. She was so full of energy he was surprised her hair hadn't started smoking. He maneuvered his way past several unfamiliar faces to the bagels and coffee laid out. After slathering a garlic bagel with salsa cream cheese and grabbing a black coffee, he turned back to find her not-so-quietly vibrating in place behind him.

"What's the story, Angie?" he asked.

"Funny you should ask that," she said grinning, "because we're about to talk about the story right now."

A petite woman he hadn't noticed rose smoothly from the table and approached him, hand extended. Her dark eyes studied him as he shook her hand, taking in his appearance—his T-shirt and jeans a stark contrast to her own refined, if exotic, clothing. A light-colored silk blouse and loose pants complemented by the discrete diamond sparkling on the side of her nose made her look like a modern-day Indian princess. Her voice, when she spoke, was smooth and cadenced with only a slight lilt of an accent.

"You must be Max," she said. "It is a pleasure to meet you. I'm Manisha, Virtual Undead storyteller."

She started laughing almost immediately. "I can see by the look on your face that you don't use storytellers here."

© Rebecca Baker and CA 2017
R. Baker, *Agile UX Storytelling*, DOI 10.1007/978-1-4842-2997-2_2

Max blushed, chagrined at what must have been obvious scorn on his face. Thankfully, Manisha didn't seem to have taken offense. He could see Angie over her shoulder scowling at him. He looked at his feet, feeling embarrassed and a little put out.

"Well, you've got to admit, it's kind of…well, I mean 'storyteller,' right?" he muttered, trying unsuccessfully to get himself out of the hole he'd dug.

"It *is* a bit of a silly title, isn't it?" Manisha admitted, smiling at him. "But it's the best one we could come up with to describe what I do without misleading people. I'm getting ahead of myself, though—let's back up and introduce the rest of the team."

Max smiled back, relieved at her skillful redirection. Hastily he shook hands with the rest of the team Manisha had brought with her from Virtual Undead—Trevor, the UI designer; Ward, the lead developer; Ben, the researcher; Jolene, the product manager; and Colleen, the support manager. The main portion of the development, support, and QA teams were touring the offices as was the sales team.

"So," Manisha started, "you've heard a little bit about the acquisition this morning, yes?"

"Just that there has been one, nothing more than that." Max said, looking a bit accusingly at Angie. She studiously ignored him, concentrating on her bagel as if it were the most delicious thing she'd ever tasted. Manisha glanced at her and, seeing no move to interrupt, continued.

"To catch you up on what we do, Virtual Undead's software simulates zombie movements at a step-by-step—or as we like to call it stagger-by-stagger—level through augmented reality glasses. We use modeling algorithms to predict next moves, which lets elimination experts anticipate and improve efficiency." She paused, making sure he was following.

"So, you make it easier to shoot zombies?" Max confirmed. Manisha nodded.

"Exactly. But only on a zombie-by-zombie basis. That's where your software comes in. As you know, Where's The Zombie tracks macro movements of the undead, predicting swarms and risings. Combining the two gives us an end-to-end solution to tracking. Plus, mining the combined data is highly likely to improve the efficacy of our algorithms.

But there's an even more immediate opportunity. The government needs tracking software that can integrate with the targeting system of the army's new weapon." She stopped, looking at Angie again. The CEO nodded for her to continue. Taking a deep breath, Manisha said, "Unfortunately, the proof of concept for the RFP is due in one month."

Max nearly choked on his bagel. After scalding his mouth on the coffee in an attempt to get the rest of the bagel down, he sputtered, "One *month*? To integrate two completely different code bases with a hardware interface? And that doesn't even begin to touch on the workflow integration for a system that has to be field-ready for God-only-knows what user base? Are you *insane?*"

The lead developer barked a laugh, which turned into a cough as Ben elbowed his ribs. Manisha nodded her head sympathetically. "I know it's a lot to take in, but I'm confident that with our combined expertise, some good research, and a story, we'll be able to come up with proof of concept that will not only satisfy the government requirements but give us the blueprint we need to make a really great product."

Max just stared at her open-mouthed. She didn't seem like a crazy person, but what she just said was, without a doubt, crazy.

Angie snickered. "Close your mouth, Max, before you start catching flies!"

Manisha smiled, nodding to the whiteboard wall behind him. "Let me explain how stories are going to help us."

She walked up to the wall, snagging a marker on her way past the table. She started to draw as she talked.

"Since humans first started to communicate, they have done so in stories."

She drew two stick figures facing each other.

"Stories give us not just the facts but how the person telling the story sees those facts. They give us context." She gave each person a thought bubble—one had a circle in it, the other a square.

Then the person with the circle started talking and the listener had a thought bubble that had square = circle.

"By telling each other stories, we are able to see things from other people's perspectives and help other people see our perspective."

"This lets us come to a common understanding and move forward."

She drew two figures again with a square with rounded corners, replacing the contents of the thought bubbles with the same shape.

"Stories also help us understand patterns."

Now she drew two new stick figures. One had a speech bubble with three stars, one circle, and three more stars. The other had a thought bubble with three stars, one circle, three stars, one circle, and then three dots.

"...even if we can't see the patterns ourselves," she finished.

Max nodded his head reluctantly. "OK, that's all nice but how is that going to make this insanity Angie has cooked up doable?"

Manisha erased her drawings and wrote "Problem" as high as she could reach. It was not very high. Then she turned to Max, "To tell a story, first you need to know the problem that the characters are trying to solve. So, let's talk about what our problem is."

Max leaned back, thinking. This was a lot like some of the design sprints[1] they had run at the game studio he'd worked at prior to Where's The Zombie. You had to define the problem before you could get on with the solution.

"OK, talk me through the problem."

Manisha took a moment to take a drink from her thermos before continuing. The elaborate scrollwork on the metal seemed a stark and artful contrast to the somewhat sterile conference table, and Max wondered what she was drinking. Tea? If he had to bet, he would bet it was tea.

---

[1] The Design Sprint, www.gv.com/sprint/.

"We have several problems," Manisha said, returning to the whiteboard. "Let's start with how we're defining problems."

She continued, "For our purpose, a problem is a situation or event that we want to change to achieve a different result. The problem definition should include both the problem statement—that is, what the situation or event is—as well as the desired result. The important thing is to avoid trying to solve the problem in the problem definition."

Max nodded vigorously, glancing sidelong at Angie. She was studying her shoes, deliberately not looking up. This was an old argument they'd had many times—she had a tendency to want to jump straight into problem-solving mode and had a hard time understanding why that was an issue.

"Exactly," Max said, "it's like asking someone to build you a car instead of asking them to build you a way to transport individuals and their belongings from one point to another."

Manisha smiled again. "Precisely. By defining the problem, you determine all of the requirements. In your example, you would need to define how many individuals would need to be transported at one time, under what circumstances, how frequently, and so on."

"But," Angie interjected looking a bit miffed, "then you might design a bicycle or a scooter or something! And I wanted a car!"

"Do you?" Manisha asked, unperturbed by the interruption. "By defining your requirements well without suggesting a solution, you might end up getting a teleportation device or something equally amazing. There are a number of excellent examples of how well-defined problems lead to superior solutions, from the oil industry to medical research.[2] Defining a problem well is both difficult and rewarding. It can lead to true innovation or could identify new directions. It ensures that you do not create a solution in search of a problem.

"At Virtual Zombie, we've discovered that creating stories helps us better define problems. Let me show you what I mean."

On the board, she drew three large squares, like a cartoon series. In the first, she drew a stick figure with its hands in the air and a thought bubble that said, "Oh no…zombies!" with another angry-looking stick figure reaching for it. In the second square, she drew the same two figures, with a third pointing a gun with the label "new" at the zombie saying "I'll save you!" The third box had the zombie sticking its tongue out at the figure with the gun saying "Missed me sucker!"

---

[2]Dwayne Spradlin, "The Power of Defining the Problem," *Harvard Business Review*, September 25, 2012, https://hbr.org/2012/09/the-power-of-defining-the-prob.

Max snorted. "So our problem is that zombies are sassy?"

Manisha laughed. "If only! Our problem is that we need to protect people from zombies. We want to use the government's invention, but the new weapon does not do a good job of targeting. It's not very mobile or easy to use, like a rifle or a handgun."

Intrigued, Max asked, "What are the specifications?"

"Good question!" Jolene slid a stack of papers over to him. Justin scooted a chair over to take a look. Max started reading through the papers. The weapon was unwieldy and heavy—it had to be mounted on something that could move it around. Accuracy was important for disruption of the zombie, but shooting innocent civilians wouldn't be an issue as the pulse was not harmful to regular humans.

Justin looked up. "So, why don't they just widen the beam? It says here that tests on humans showed no reaction—why not just make it like a big area effect?"

Jolene nodded at the papers. "Keep reading."

Max had already reached the answer. "Look here," he pointed to a diagram, "its effectiveness becomes diluted as the beam becomes larger. Larger than a basketball, and it becomes useless. It's got to be...let's see...2 inches in diameter for optimal effect." He looked up at Manisha and Jolene in surprise. "That's tight! How accurate can you be with the VZ software?"

The lead developer, a young man with long dark hair, spoke up. Max tried to remember his name...Winston? Wesley? William? Definitely a W-something....

"Accuracy won't be the issue in a single case—it's scaling it to large groups that require retargeting that hits our limit. We can model singular zombie movements to within tolerance."

Manisha moved back to the board, and under "Problem" she wrote "protect humans from zombies." Under that she started a bulleted list titled

"Requirements." To it she added "use government weapon," "retargeting" and "accuracy to 2 inches."

PROBLEM:

PROTECT HUMANS FROM ZOMBIES

Requirements:
- use government weapon
- retargeting
- accuracy to 2 inches

"There's more, of course," she said. "This has to be operated in the field—that's implied here, but it has repercussions for the solution."

Max nodded. "Right, we'll need to consider environmental factors such as lighting and weather."

"Precisely!" Manisha said, adding "account for variable lighting/weather" to the list. "What else?"

"Well…," Angie said slowly, "I imagine it will be used in the field, so a fair amount of psychological stress?" She looked embarrassed as she said it.

"Yes!" Manisha said, encouraging her. "This has to be simple because it will be used in a combat situation. We cannot rely on the user to think too much about how to use this." She wrote "simple operation" on the board.

Stepping back, she looked at the group and started speaking, "A deader squad is in a high-rise that has been recently infected. They're trying to clear floor by floor, but there are still uninfected humans inside. Zombies and humans both come toward them but for very different reasons. The power in the building went out earlier because of an ill-advised panicky decision on the part of building management, and only the emergency lighting is on. It's flickering and shadowy, and there are screams everywhere. The team of five has to clear all fifty floors before they can stand down and have a well-deserved beer." She took a deep breath, letting it out slowly.

"Ladies and gentlemen, this is our story."

Key Takeaways

- Stories can accelerate software development by

    - Improving communication. Stories ensure everyone is sharing a perspective.

    - Defining the problem. By spending time up front adequately defining the problem and requirements, less time is spent later in the cycle (where it becomes more expensive in time and money).

- Defining problems before solutions is essential to encourage innovation. Starting off by defining a solution as part of the problem ("Make me a car") limits the solutions you can come up with.

- Defining problems is difficult. Solutions are satisfying, and it is easy to jump straight to solutions. It is important to resist this urge to improve the ability of the team to innovate.

- Defining problems is also essential for adequate requirements gathering. Jumping to solutions too early can lead to missed requirements, which turns into rework later in the process.

The Plan

The room was quiet, absorbing the short but compelling story. Max was starting to see how this would help.

"So…," he said slowly, "we use the stories to help us all understand on a visceral level what we're doing and why."

"Exactly." It was Trevor, Virtual Zombie's designer, who spoke up. His deep brown eyes darted to Manisha for confirmation. She smiled encouragingly, so he kept going. "The story makes us think about things in context and in entirety, not in pieces. We'll break it into pieces later, but really those are just like little vignettes that are part of the whole story."

"Notice the story she just told us doesn't have a conclusion," said Ben, the Virtual Zombie researcher. "That's because, like we talked about earlier, we're just coming up with the problem first. So, no solution. Also, it is only the start. We need more stories that represent use cases, requirements for the end result, and scope." Heads around the table nodded in understanding. "We can get a lot of this from the RFP and what we know about the space, but we'll need to do some investigative work as well."

"Got it." Max started thinking. "So, what we need to know next is—"

He was interrupted as Sylvia burst into the room. Geoffrey ambled behind in her wake, swept along with the tide. A large woman with a severely short dark bob who enjoyed dressing in bold colors, Sylvia moved like a tank on military maneuvers, dominating the space and forcing others to step back to make room. She lurched to a stop in front of Max.

© Rebecca Baker and CA 2017
R. Baker, *Agile UX Storytelling*, DOI 10.1007/978-1-4842-2997-2_3

"What. The. Hell?" she asked in a dangerously quiet voice.

"Hi, Sylvia! How are you doing this morning? Where have you been?" Max smiled, watching her scowl deepen further. Really, he probably shouldn't bait her—she could easily squash him—but with an entrance like that....

"How am I doing?" She growled. "How do you *think* I am doing? I get in this morning as usual, and Justin"—her eyes swiveled to find the product manager in question, all but cowering behind his coffee cup—"informs me that we have acquired another company and 'have I seen you around?'" She took a deep breath. "*Not the best start to my day, I'd say.*"

Geoffrey sidled up behind her, "I dunno—I'd say it's a pretty awesome start. Keeping things fresh." His voice, surprisingly deep, made Max's grin widen. In contrast to Sylvia, he was painfully slender, and his clothes—a uniform of black T-shirts and khakis—were the very nature of office camouflage. His voice always surprised people, less for its quality and more for the rarity of hearing it. "And as for where we've been," he looked pointedly at Justin who was continuing to pretend the conversation wasn't happening, "Justin was supposed to come get us. We saw the tour group come through and figured we better come find you."

"Well, glad you're here. I told you it'd never be dull, didn't I?" Max gestured around the room. "Sylvia, Geoffrey, I'd like to introduce you to the Virtual Zombie team." He introduced each of the members, giving Sylvia a chance to process and cool down. As she shook each hand, he could see her relaxing visibly.

"We were just starting by identifying the story. So, your timing is great." Manisha gestured toward the board. "Our research team will need to take the lead on some rapid fact finding to fill out some of our setting and character details."

Sylvia looked surprised. "You're a storyteller? I've been reading about those. How long have you been doing this?"

"Three years, give or take," Manisha replied. "But I'm still learning more every day. It's a constantly evolving approach."

"So, what's our story?"

Manisha restated the story and then quickly wrote on the whiteboard.

CONTEXT	+ CONFOUND	+ TO DO	+ RESULT
Choose common situation w/most limiting factors	Need to do "x" with "Y" limitations	Characters must do "X"	Desired resolution (-solution) to confound listing

"This is the form our problem stories follow. We started with the problem statement and base requirements. Now we have it in the form of an overarching context with a human—and zombie—face." She paused, looking around the room before going on. "Next, we need to work on creating specific, supporting stories that will inform our research efforts and direction for the product. What questions do we need answered?"

Max watched as Sylvia pulled up a chair and sat, eyes never leaving the whiteboard. He could practically hear the gears turning in her head as she absorbed every detail. He'd been surprised she knew about storytellers, but on reflection he supposed he shouldn't be. Sylvia was a voracious reader and rarely unaware of any trend in the industry.

"We need to flesh out the characters; observe the weaponry in use to understand any unstated limitations, requirements, and scope; and then determine what our happy ending looks like. Ben, can you walk us through the character creation so we can unpack that?"

Ben unfolded from his seat and strode to the whiteboard, accepting the marker from Manisha. He started by writing "Characters" near the top of the whiteboard. Max noticed it was a good foot higher than Manisha's "Problem."

"Using the story, we can identify three explicit characters who need to be mapped and one implied. The explicit characters are, of course, the squad members who will be the direct users of the product, the uninfected nonmilitary humans who will not interact directly with the product but will benefit from it and may react to its use in unpredictable ways, and the zombies that will be the target of the product."

Reaching up, he wrote "Explicit" under "Characters" and listed each of the characters, each with its own stick figure.

CHARACTERS

Explicit:

① SQUAD ② HUMANS ③ ZOMBIES ④ WEAPONS

"We also consider software and hardware 'characters' for this exercise so we can keep them in context, that is, within the setting or environment of the story." He listed the weapon and each type of software next.

"Implicit characters are those implied by the narrative but not directly mentioned. In this case we have implied that they have the equipment they need to do the job, so there is an implied outfitter who would have provided and configured the product for the team before the team enters the situation." Then Ben nodded to the list under "Problems" and said, "Also, I want to point out that we have made the implied assumption, through what *isn't* on the requirements list, that field configuration is not currently on the table for the RFP."

Trevor spoke up. "Maybe not, but it's a good point—we need to make sure we have an alternate timeline that handles that so we keep it in mind for future iterations."

Everyone started talking at once. Max stayed quiet trying to decide what kind of whacky science-fiction "alternate timeline" would take them down.

Ben raised his voice, "Folks, hang on, one at a time! Trevor, you're right, we should start notes for an alternate timeline. So we're on the same page, an alternate timeline is what we call stories that cover features we want to consider including but aren't part of our scope for a given release. They are things that we need to keep in mind to provide room for them in the future. They keep us from inadvertently boxing ourselves into a solution that isn't extensible or losing ideas that come to light during ideation." He looked around the room, a bit sheepish. "I know it's a bit goofy. We're all big science-fiction fans, and it just seemed to fit. But really, it's just a way to keep stories that are outside of scope in our peripheral view. We're not building an alternate dimension that will take us to a parallel universe or anything."

On the whiteboard, he wrote "Implicit" and listed the outfitter with his own stick figure. Next to that he wrote "Alternates" and started a bulleted list with "Field configuration" as the first item.

"Now wait," Max said, thinking out loud. "There could be an infinite number of rabbit holes we run down with this. How do we keep it from getting crazy? I don't want to end up putting a cup holder on this thing because someone might want a cold one in the middle of a shoot-out!"

The room laughed, and Ben, smiling broadly, nodded. "Great question! You don't really need to keep them in line from a practical standpoint because we're not actually going to do anything with them at the moment. So if you have a crazy what-if idea, we write it down to acknowledge it. That's the important part. It's a way not only to keep things in mind but also to clear the board so we can concentrate on what we have to do for the current problem."

Max sat back, crossing his arms. "OK, let's see how this goes."

Ben turned back to the board. "Now that we've identified the characters and started an alternate timeline, or list of alternate stories, we need to determine how much we know. Let's list the unknowns."

He continued, "This is a new weapon system, so the usage is completely unknown." Next to the weapon system he drew a circle and colored it in completely.

"Next we have the zombies. Zombie behavior in these situations is pretty predictable, at least for our software. Otherwise we'd all be out of jobs!" A smattering of laughter greeted this assertion. He drew a circle next to the zombie that was not colored in at all. "Same with our software," he added.

"But the shooters and outfitter are both new personas for us, so we need to see how they work—what environment are they operating in and what types of interactions they're currently dealing with within the context of our story. We don't need a complete picture of what they're doing when not on a mission." Squad had a half-colored-in circle.

"The noninfected folks need to be researched from a tangential point of view—we can rely on some interviews with squad members who have been through these types of situations and don't need to do direct observations." The noninfected happy stick figure got a circle with a quarter of it colored in.

① SQUAD   **② HUMANS**

③ ZOMBIES   **④ WEAPONS**

"Using this, we can easily see we know the least about the weapon system, squad members, and the outfitter. The question is, what do we need to know about those things and people, and how will we use that information to inform what we create?"

"Well," Angie said, "we need to know a lot about the weapon system. I mean, we need lots of details, and the RFP doesn't provide nearly enough." She hopped down from the table and started pacing. "The problem story captures some of the main requirements, but not all of them. I need to know if the RFP matches reality."

Ben nodded, "OK, so a broad exploration on the weapon to get more information all around. We don't know enough to drill down into it yet."

Angie bounced her head in agreement. "Right! Fortunately, I got a call back this morning from our government contact, and we should be able to have a demo tomorrow afternoon."

Sylvia looked taken aback. "That was quick!"

"Yeah, I was a bit surprised too," Angie said. "But with the short time lines, it makes sense."

Ben interjected, "Any chance of some time with the folks operating the weapon after the demo?"

"Yes," Angie said, "I've asked for interviews with people on the first squad that will be an early adopter of the weapon after the demo."

"What do we want to know from them?" Sylvia asked pointedly. "We need more direction if we're going to make good use of their time."

"Current challenges using the weapon," Max said. "Environmental issues that might not be apparent during the demo but could affect our solution."

"Are there other people who need to use this other than the squad members?" Geoffrey added. "Like noncombat personnel?"

Sylvia made some quick notes.

"Good points," Manisha said, stepping in. "Is there anything else we could do to add clarity? Come up with more questions?"

Sylvia glanced up at the board and then to Ben. "What about the weapons integration research—looking for information on how this has been done before, what the technical challenges are going to be in getting our software to talk to the weapon system, and so on."

Manisha nodded her agreement. "Our development team has done a number of integration explorations, including an integration with Zinko last year, so we've got a lot of what we'll need already. Ward, can you set up a cloud drop for everyone?"

"Sure thing!" Ward replied. "Let me go sync up with the rest of the team. I think they're still touring the floor."

"They're probably stalled in the coffee room—someone brought cookies in this morning," Angie said, waving her hands about. "I'll take you to them."

Max was pensive as they left. Things were definitely moving fast, but would it be fast enough? And they still had only one story. He didn't see how this would work. Just then he remembered the zombie from the morning.

"Oh!" he blurted out, catching a look from several of the people still in the room. "I almost forgot. Justin, I saw something today that may blow our movement algorithms out of the water." He told a wide-eyed room about the zombie that ran and the van with the people in biohazard suits.

"Maybe he wasn't a zombie? Maybe he was, you know, just crazy or sick. People still get crazy and sick and aren't zombies." Justin licked his lips, thinking. "I bet that was it. It would totally explain the van and everything. You're just so used to seeing zombies that when you saw him, your brain said 'zombie' and that was that."

"Maybe…," Max answered. But he didn't think that was the case. Something strange was up.

Key Takeaways

- Good stories can be used to help understand where you need more information and why. By identifying characters in the story, you can determine what you know and what you don't know about them, making it easier to hone in on the questions you need to answer.

- Stories that are outside the scope of the project still need to be captured and acknowledged. This technique lets you keep needs for the future in mind while designing but also lets you focus on what needs to be done right now without distraction. This approach is especially key in enterprise software because, due to the scale you are working with, you consistently have to define a tight minimum viable product while still leaving room for significant growth in the near future.

- Research can be exploratory or specific in nature. However, it is important to know what you are trying to find out for it to be effective. Understand what you are looking for before you start to look.

A Visit

Most of the group filed out of the conference room, leaving Manisha, Max, and Justin behind. Angie sidled back in, perching on the table. Manisha looked over at Max, cocking her head to one side.

"Penny for your thoughts," she said.

Max cleared his throat, trying to put his misgivings into words. "It's a lot of moving parts with very little information," he said finally. "I can see how we've got an ideal case, but there's so much we don't know."

"Exactly!" Justin nearly shouted his interruption, making Max and Manisha jump. "This is a total shot in the dark! How can you just make up a story like that and expect us to believe it will work? I mean, where's the research? We should be planning this for months before we try to make a move! We don't know if it will work at all. This isn't part of our core—this isn't what we do. And you just expect us to jump into it eyes closed, feet first, with a great big smile on our faces? You're nuts! I won't do it! It's a disaster waiting to happen!"

Manisha waited for Justin to wind down before smiling and reaching over to touch his hand. "That's an interesting perspective. Tell me, what information do you feel like is missing?"

Justin spluttered, gesticulating wildly in the air as he jerked away from her. "Market analysis! Problem verification! System compatibility!" He jumped up from his seat and started to pace. "I mean, sure, it's an RFP, so the market is pretty locked down I guess. But problem verification is huge—you said yourself we need to keep it open-ended to make sure we're solving the real problem, not what they *imagine* the problem is. And that takes time we just don't have. I don't see how we can get that to a high degree of confidence before we have to start coding the proof of concept. And then the system

© Rebecca Baker and CA 2017
R. Baker, *Agile UX Storytelling*, DOI 10.1007/978-1-4842-2997-2_4

compatibility issues! What if we can't make our software talk to each other? What if we can't make it talk to the firmware the weapon has installed? What if...," he trailed off as he looked over at Angie. Max turned to see a slightly guilty smile on her face.

Justin stared. "Angie?"

She shrugged from where she sat, perched on the table. "Hey, you guys didn't think I made this decision in a vacuum did you? We did our due diligence prior to the acquisition. Have some faith in Owen and Ward—they're smart guys. The firmware interface is another matter, but we're doing investigations on that as we speak." She turned to face them both. "Guys, this is an opportunity—a *huge* opportunity. And we are in a position to move quickly and take advantage of it. I know it seems fast, but we've all done things like this before. I'll admit that there's a risk. But it's a calculated risk, not a foolhardy one. I need you both to get your running shoes on and stop bellyaching about the fact that I moved your cheese."[1] She hopped down and started walking toward the door. "You know your stuff—you got this." And then she was gone.

Max stared open-mouthed at the empty doorway before shaking himself and turning back to Justin and Manisha.

"Worst. Pep talk. Ever!" he said with a shake of his head. "She might be right, of course. I'm totally caught off guard by all of this."

Manisha smiled and nodded her understanding. "I think just telling you to trust is a bit much. The two companies have been looking at merging for a while, and this RFP was the tipping point. We have stories for the business cases that we explored." She smiled at Max's expression. "Oh, yeah, we do stories for those too. I've been involved since the beginning, so all of this is a lot less of a surprise to me. I definitely understand how disconcerting all this can be."

Justin crossed his arms with a frown. "Yeah, well, 'disconcerting' is sugar-coating it. I'd say fu...."

"Justin!" Max interrupted, cutting his eyes at Manisha.

"What? I can't even express an opinion anymore? Screw that! I'm out of here!" Justin stomped out of the room, muttering under his breath.

Max sighed. "He'll cool down in an hour or two. This product is his baby, and he just needs some time to get used to the idea. And Angie isn't helping." He paused. "But he's right that we've just got the happy path. How do we account for the not-so-happy paths? Also, you said we have business cases? I'd like to see those."

---

[1] Spencer Johnson, *Who Moved My Cheese* (GP Putnam Sons, 1988).

Manisha nodded. "Absolutely. I'll send them to you right now." She turned to her laptop, typing furiously for a moment and then turned back to him. "There! And for the not-so-happy paths we have horror stories. We should be able to knock out a few of them now. We'll be able to get more once the research team gets back with the contextual work so we have a better understanding of the current challenges." She reached for the whiteboard marker and started a new list titled "Trouble."

"First, let's list potential failure points we'll need to consider. Off the top of my head there's visibility—the risk that they cannot see the targeting screen because of lighting conditions. Equipment failure—how do we handle an error within the hardware or software?"

Max chimed in, "Multiple targets, multiple users…oh, wait, that's not so much a failure point as a use case."

Manisha started a second list title of "Use Cases." She said, "Exactly. And we need to capture those too. Keep 'em coming."

After about 15 minutes they had added environmental factors (rain, cold, heat, etc.) and interference (enemy control of weapon) to their failure points. The use cases were proving harder.

"I just don't have a good feel for the workflow on this," Max grumbled. "And how are we going to turn this into…what did you call it? Horror stories?"

Manisha laughed. "Again, it's not as hard as it seems. Let's take visibility, for example. We need to make stories that cover using the system when it is very bright, very dark, or the person using it is otherwise unable to see the interface." She paused for a moment. "Take our original story, the deader squad in the high-rise. You'll remember the power is out, and it's poorly lit. Now, let's add a line to the story about the gunner for this weapon. He wears prescription glasses, and in the initial rush into the building they are knocked off his head and break."

Max sighed. "Sounds a bit hokey, but OK, I'm game. So, he can't see well both because of lighting and because of losing his glasses."

Manisha nodded. "Once we get everyone back together, we can test that scenario out and see whether it holds. If it does, we write requirements for eyes-free operation."

Max was unconvinced. "Look, I don't want to be disrespectful, but it seems to me that this is a lot of extra window dressing without a good return. I mean, I like a good story as much as anyone! I'm just not getting it."

Manisha just nodded, unperturbed by his doubt. "I know, it's hard to see the value at first. It seems silly and like extra work for no reason. The return comes when you get multiple people involved. That's when you need stories the most. It keeps everyone on the same page and ensures you're seeing things the same way—or at least know that you are not seeing things the same way."[2] She paused, thinking. "Have you ever designed something perfectly to Justin's specifications but had him come back and tell you that wasn't what he asked for?"

Max looked down, a bit uncomfortable. "Well, sure. All the designers I know have that problem. Product managers are just...well, they aren't always that good at writing requirements, you know? Plus they're always coming up with new stuff to push into it and...," he trailed off, starting to understand.

Manisha prompted, "And it's like they aren't on the same page as you? Like they have a different idea in their head?"

Nodding slowly, Max conceded, "Just like that. I'm not totally convinced stories will help that, but I guess I'm willing to try." He looked back at the board. "I just wish I had a better grasp of the use cases. I want to get moving on this. We'll see what the research team comes up with. Meanwhile, we might as well get moving on our own part of the research by looking at potential competitors." He paused. "Where'd Trevor go? He's going to want to be in on this."

Manisha pulled out her phone. "I'll text him—he's probably scoping out the break room for caffeine."

While he waited, Max studied the four business cases that Manisha sent him. The first two dealt with integrations of the Where's The Zombie and Virtual Zombie software to try to get into the market in Africa. Because of the current economic challenges in the region, most of the African governments were dealing with the zombie threat via drones. However, their accuracy left much to be desired, and civilian casualties were often high. By integrating the two approaches, they would provide a new method of drone targeting. Max nodded to himself as he skimmed through them, thinking about the opportunities they outlined. The third business case dealt with aggregating the data from the two companies to look for patterns in zombie risings and movements. It was clearly a work in progress, with sections missing and comments peppering the margins (such as "willingness to pay?" and "need more data"). The last business case was for the RFP. It had been pulled together hastily, drawing from the African business case, but altered to take into account the government requirements. The two most interesting parts were the risk assessment and the narrative. The risk assessment outlined most of the issues he already knew about—mainly the lack of details in the RFP and the potential technical problems with having their software integrate with the weapon hardware. But it also listed one he wasn't aware of—competitors. The information about the other bidders was spotty, but it appeared there were at least two big companies that

---

[2]Lori Silverman, *Wake Me Up When the Data Is Over: How Organizations Use Stories to Drive Results* (Wiley, 2006).

were expected to compete for the contract: ORKON International Weapons and Trisec Security. The narrative was part of the executive summary. He read through it with interest; it was quite close to the story they had come up with this morning but with more results. It tied the specifics in the business case together.

"Justin says he's coming," Manisha said, interrupting his reading.

"OK, then let's start our initial search work."

Max pulled up another browser tab and started searching for *weapon software interface*. Results quickly filled his screen, and he read through the first few.

- "Weapon store management: Inventory control for weapons store"
- "Ration Software integrates older air weapons with drones, FAAC reports"
- "ORKON International weapons systems: Integration of modern-day weapons with cutting-edge technology"
- "Launcher and weapon interoperability—common interfaces: RFP for study on instituting a common interface for weapons launch software"

He felt Manisha pull up a chair behind him. She smelled like spiced tea and apples, making him think incongruously of his autumns on campus as a student at MIT. He mentally shook himself free of the odd memory.

"Competitive analysis? Good call," she said, reading over his shoulder. "Check out the ORKON system. They'll be competing with us for sure."

Max pulled up the ORKON site. Their landing page was impressive—slick background videos showed soldiers in Augmented Reality (AR) goggles stalking through targets and shooting them with complete accuracy. Testimonials and Point of View (POV) videos of the software filled the page.

Manisha nodded at the information. "Good setup for a mobile solution, but the AR isn't really necessary for targeting with the weapon system as we understand it. It'd be cool, but not effective."

"Agreed. But remember, we still don't know if the weapon system description is accurate. We should still include it," Max said, making some notes and returning to his search. Next he brought up the study on launcher and weapon interoperability. The paper had a lengthy description of the study parameters, as well as some interesting diagrams showing key areas of consideration when providing targeting displays for weapons use.

display_02: `cluster`

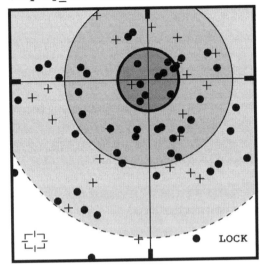

target cluster:
optimize area
destruction

broad scope:
increase reach
to secondary
targets

display_01: `individual`

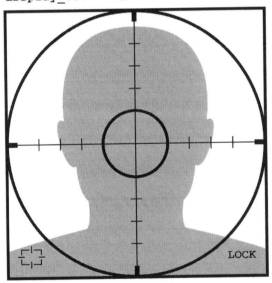

target lock:
improved
precision

tight scope:
limit field
distraction

Trevor walked in and set his laptop down beside Max's. After a couple of false starts, they had a solid list of current work, possible competitors, and highlighted items of interest from cross-over technology. Unsurprisingly, several gaming interfaces featured on the list, highlighting interactive styles and techniques that could prove useful.

Max leaned back in his chair, stretching. "This is a good start, but—" He was cut off as alarms blared through the building. A harsh female voice repeatedly bleated over the PA system: "Alert! Alert! Zombie detected on your floor. Secure doors. Alert! Alert! This is not a drill."

Max sprang out of his chair, snapping the laptop shut. Trevor sprinted to the conference room door and locked it with a quick twist. All three designers moved to the back of the room, as far away from the door as possible, and sat down on the floor, out of sight. Shouts in the hall. Slamming doors. Then quiet except the blaring of the alert system.

Max felt cold sweat slide down his neck, making him shiver slightly. His stomach was in knots. This wasn't supposed to happen. His gun was in the car, but it might as well have been a million miles away. When was the last time he practiced at the range? He silently cursed his procrastination. Situational preparedness is what his dad would've said. And the old man would've laughed at him for being caught with his pants down like this. He felt stupid.

Max glanced over at Trevor and Manisha. Both looked nervous and frightened. Like fire drills, zombie drills were a regular part of everyone's safety training. No one wondered what to do or where to go—they just did it. But just like fires, zombie incursions were rare. And the real thing was scary. The alert system cut off, leaving an eerie silence.

Loud in the sudden hush, the door handle to the conference room rattled, making them all jump. Voices low and hushed and urgent in tone followed. They were too soft to understand the words, but the intent seeped through—*hurry*. Shouts and the sound of running feet. Then quiet. Long minutes ticked by.

Suddenly the loud speaker blared: "Undead threat secured. You may return to your desks. Undead threat secured. You may return to your desks."

Trevor shook himself slightly as he pushed up off the floor. "Well," he said with a shaky laugh, "if I needed to get some field experience on this one, I think that just did it for me!"

Max nodded, walking over to the door and cautiously unlocking it. He looked up and down the hallway and out into the open cubicle area, but the office seemed empty. He could hear people starting to come out of conference rooms around the corner. No sign of who had tried the door or their pursuers.

Abruptly Justin appeared, racing around the corner and startling Max who dropped the phone he'd been holding. Wild-eyed, he grabbed Max by the shoulders, studying his face intently.

"You're OK. Tell me you're OK!" he panted. Max could feel the man's hands shaking where they gripped him.

"Hey, yeah, calm down. I'm OK. Really. It's cool, man."

Justin abruptly let go. Max had never seen him so freaked out before.

"That's it, we can't do this. We've got to tell Angie the deal is off; we're out."

Max stepped back, confused. "Justin, I'm as freaked out as anyone, but this didn't have anything to do with the RFP."

Justin shook his head emphatically. "Are you sure? Seems like a hell of a coincidence to me. How much do we know about—" Suddenly, he stopped talking and stared over Max's shoulder. Max turned to find Manisha in the doorway. The look on her face was unreadable. He turned back to find Justin stone-faced.

"Look—" Max started.

Justin interrupted him. "I've got to go." He turned and all but ran back down the hallway. Max stared after him a moment before turning to Manisha. Silently she handed him his dropped phone.

"Thanks," he managed. She nodded and then turned to go back into the conference room. He sighed. This project had enough problems without Justin's weird behavior. What on Earth had gotten in to him? He made a mental note to give his friend a call when they finished the competitive research and see whether they could get a drink at the Hollow Tree pub. Maybe he'd calm down after a beer or two.

Key Takeaways

- Stories apply to all segments of software development, including product management. Business cases can easily be crafted into stories to help illustrate a point and to ensure that the original goal of the business case persists throughout the software development process. For a good resource on creating business cases, see Ray Sheen and Amy Gallo's *Teach Yourself: Building a Business Case* (Harvard Business Review, 2015).

- Competitive analysis is traditionally the realm of product but is also useful in design. For design it has two distinct parts. In the first, designers look for inspiration and context by seeing how others in the same or near spaces have solved the problem. For example, a designer trying to solve the problem of the best interface for dog adoption might review other adoption web sites, but they would also look at Tinder to understand matching patterns and at Amazon to understand checkout flows. The second part is a more rigorous analysis of strengths and weaknesses from the user experience standpoint. This approach parallels the product management Strength Weakness Opportunity Threat analysis but focuses on the UX of the product rather than the market positioning. This type of competitive analysis is used when looking for parity or a competitive edge when entering a space with significant competition. For more information on conducting a competitive analysis, see Danforth Media's "Conducting a Solid UX Competitive Analysis" at http://danforth.co/pages/2014/03/01/conducting-a-solid-ux-competitive-analysis/.

CHAPTER

5

Field Work

The sterile office/waiting room that prefaced the weapons test warehouse gave a new definition to the word *frigid*. Sylvia shivered, wrapping her thin sweater even tighter around her in an attempt to stave off hypothermia. Sitting next to her on an identically uncomfortable metal chair, Ben seemed unaffected by the cold. His fingers tapped rhythmically on his tablet cover while he looked around the room—not that there was a lot to see. Aside from a gray metal desk with a perpetually angry-looking man dressed in army khakis behind it and two other punishing metal chairs, there was nothing in the room. No display, no table of pamphlets, nothing. Sylvia wondered, not for the first time, if this was some type of elaborate joke. She wouldn't put it past Max. It'd be just like him and that obnoxious product manager Justin to cook up a stupid scheme to get her "more involved." She glared suspiciously at Ben—he could be an actor, hired to play the part of a fellow researcher. She tried to think of a question that would expose his identity as a fake. The man next to her seemed oblivious to her scrutiny. He even had an annoyingly cheerful air about him, like he was about to go on a grand adventure.

"So," she started, her teeth almost chattering as she spoke, "I was wondering—"

"You Ben?" a booming voice echoed through the room, making her jump.

Ben jumped up extending his hand to the bear of a man who had entered the room. Middle-aged, muscular, sandy blond hair cropped close to his scalp and bright blue eyes, he seemed to take up more space than should be possible for one person. He shook hands with Ben, clapping him roughly on the shoulder, and then turned to her, smiling.

© Rebecca Baker and CA 2017
R. Baker, *Agile UX Storytelling*, DOI 10.1007/978-1-4842-2997-2_5

"And this would be…?"

"Sylvia Thornton, lead researcher," she supplied quickly before she could be introduced. Damned if she was going to let this good ol' boys' club intimidate her. The bear man's smile faltered for just a moment at her tone but recovered almost instantaneously as he gently took her hand, squeezing it briefly.

"Sergeant Arch Caldwell, ma'am. It's a pleasure." His head inclined slightly. *If he kisses my hand, I will kill him,* Sylvia thought. He straightened, as if reading her mind, and gestured to the door at the back of the room he had come through.

"If you folks will follow me, we'll get your demo started." A slight Southern drawl marked his words. He turned and strode quickly across the room, leaving the researchers to hurriedly scurry after him. The door opened onto a large courtyard with a military jeep parked nearby. Sergeant Caldwell was already in the jeep when they emerged from the door, and they both clambered in with him, Sylvia in the front seat and Ben hopping in the back. As soon as Ben sat, the sergeant shifted into drive, tearing away from the building at a slightly alarming speed. Sylvia tried not to clutch at her seat as the jeep hit a bump and she felt herself flying up. They drove out of the courtyard and into a field with something that might be called a road, if you were feeling generous, leading up a slight hill. As they crested the hill, she could see a large fenced area. It looked like there were people moving around inside the fence and some outside, although there was something odd about how they were moving. As they drove closer, she realized why, and her stomach started to churn—the people inside the fence weren't people. They were zombies.

"I…I…I thought this was just a demo," she stammered. She glanced back at Ben who was looking a little green. At least it wasn't just her.

"Yes ma'am. Can't demo a weapon without a target, can we?" Sergeant Caldwell seemed completely unaware of his passenger's uneasiness. Sylvia couldn't think of anything to say to that, so she sat quietly. She'd seen zombies on video, of course, but never in person. Geoffrey had texted her last night about a zombie incident at the office that had happened after she'd left. Of course, Geoffrey just thought it was "cool." Typical. She, on the other hand, had a quiet freak-out about a zombie wandering around where her desk was. Zombies terrified her—they were the ultimate boogey man, unreasoning, implacable, seemingly unstoppable. She had been in college when the outbreak had occurred and remembered vividly the campus lockdown, booming voices over the loud speakers claiming it was a terrorist attack. And then the screaming started. It had taken three long days to clear the campus. Three days of waiting, crouched, afraid to sleep in her dorm room. Three days of sudden terrified screams, sobbing, and silence. She still woke up in a cold sweat from dreams filled with those screams. And now she was going to be watching a monster get shot, up close and personal. She closed her eyes and started taking deep breaths, repeating reassurances to herself. *It was going to* *be OK. She was going to be OK. The zombies were behind a fence. They couldn't possibly…*the jeep hit a rock, sending her flying up from her seat again. She opened her eyes and gasped. They had reached the fence.

Half a dozen military personnel clustered around what looked like a square mirror-encrusted canon. If a mining drill and a disco ball had a torrid affair, the result would be this. Mounted on a cart with large wheels, two of the soldiers were struggling to move it a few feet closer to the fence. Inside the fence, the zombies slowly staggered toward them. She could hear the moaning now, making the skin on the back of her neck crawl. Another deep breath, and she slowly stepped out of the jeep, taking her notebook with her. Max gave her a hard time about not using a tablet, but she just preferred the feel of paper. Besides, she never ran out of batteries.

As Ben crawled out of the back, the first zombie reached the fence. It wrapped its discolored fingers around the wires and pushed experimentally. Remains of a soccer uniform hung from its shuffling form, the team logo obscured by dirt, the yellow and black stripes incongruously cheerful. Sylvia looked away and concentrated on the weapon.

Roughly 4 feet long and 1 foot in diameter, it creaked and rattled as the cart it was on was shoved across the uneven ground. Sylvia started taking notes.

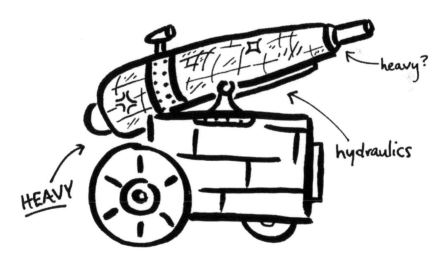

Her sketching was interrupted by a screeching sound. The weapon was starting to move. The "cart" contained some sort of hydraulic system that slowly pushed the weapon up to being even with the lead zombie's head. *I wonder how much of the weight is in the weapon and how much in the transportation hardware*, she thought. As she looked closer, she could see how heavy-duty the cart actually was. She added notes to her sketch. A tall woman brushed by her, dark hair hidden beneath her cap. She strode straight up to Ben who was positioning his tablet to take a picture of the weapon.

"No pictures, sir," she clipped. Ben lowered his tablet, flummoxed for a moment. "Security protocol."

"OK, no worries." He tucked the tablet into his messenger bag and pulled out a pen and notebook. He caught Sylvia's eye and winked at her. She rolled her eyes and got back to her sketch. She watched as the crew carefully positioned the weapon. She felt rather than saw Sergeant Caldwell come up behind her.

"The weapon—how heavy is it?" she asked.

"Maybe 10 pounds," he said. "Most of the weight is in the targeting hardware as you've noted." He tapped on the picture in the notebook. "Beastly heavy thing. Completely impractical for field use."

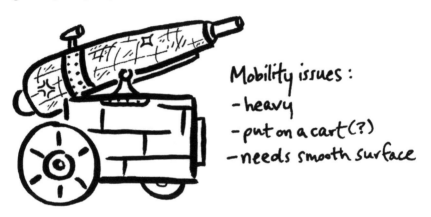

Mobility issues :
- heavy
- put on a cart (?)
- needs smooth surface

"Tell me more about the targeting hardware," she said. A technician was fiddling with dials at the back of the weapon now. Several lights came on along the sides of the weapon, rippling down the side, first orange, then yellow, then green, then finally a steady blue. The team stepped back, leaving the technician at the control. He appeared to deliberately pause and then pushed a large blue button. Rather anticlimactically, the zombie in front of the weapon collapsed in a boneless heap. Sylvia moved closer to the weapon, studying the control panel.

"The group that made the weapon didn't know sh…anything about targeting. Hardware or software," Caldwell said, following her. "They apparently thought that making it heavy would keep it steady for accuracy. Honestly, I don't see this being useful for us. Any of my squad can target deaders with 80 percent accuracy and much faster than this thing." He gave the cart a kick with his boot. "But, headquarters loves their toys."

Sylvia started sketching the control panel. It was painfully convoluted, with dials, meters, tiny obscure labels—nothing made sense. Ben was talking to the team that had pulled the weapon into place, gesturing at the zombie. She nodded to herself and whipped out a copy of the interview tool she and Ben had prepared earlier. The tool—a series of open-ended questions they had agreed on—ensured they would get the answers they needed without leaving anything out or boxing the people they talked to into a corner. She had memorized the list, of course, but she liked to bring the sheet as a reminder, as often when you started asking questions, the answers to those questions as well as the person you were talking to would change the shape and approach of your questioning. She had watched the technician working, so her questions morphed to match what she saw. "How is targeting and firing accomplished?" changed to 100 more specific questions such as "What do all these controls do, and how do you use them? What happens if the lights don't come on? What happens if you do things in the wrong order? What did you do before you walked up and started priming the weapon? What would you do now that it had fired to prepare it to fire again? What would you do if you were done firing and needed to shut it down? What other safety precautions need to be taken?" She scribbled the technician's answers frantically as slowly a picture of a very fiddly piece of equipment came to light. Even with the technician's explanations, it was still unclear what many of the controls did. The two sliders and the fourth dial dealt with the targeting system, but the first three dials had to do with prepping the charge. After turning on a hidden switch on the cart, the weapon started charging (orange), and then you turned the first dial up until it turned yellow, the second dial until it turned green, and the third until it turned blue. Then you hit the button, unless all the meters were pinged to the right, in which case you flipped the switch off and ran in the other direction.

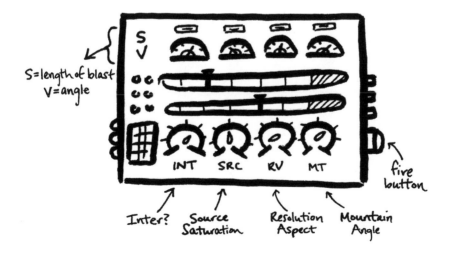

She turned to Caldwell.

"I'd like to talk to the inventors," she said briskly. Ben walked up beside her. "What's their contact information?"

Caldwell gestured for them to follow him. As they walked back to the jeep, he spoke slowly. "Good thought. Let me make a call. Are you done here?" he gestured back at his team. They were struggling to pull the weapon back from the fence toward a large truck.

Sylvia glanced at Ben, who nodded. "We'll want to do individual interviews with the team, but we can do that back at the office. If we can get—"

Boom!

The world exploded in a flash of light and sound. Orange flame rolled across the zombies gathered at the fence and the team, silencing screams and moans. Sylvia barely had time to turn before a huge hot wind slammed into her, stealing her breath and sending her flying hard into the jeep. Her head cracked against the side of the door. Then everything went black.

Key Takeaways

- Data gathering requires a particular skill set and training to be effective. Field observations, in particular, are a challenging type of ethnographic research that requires careful handling of the participants and the environment to control for bias, ensure complete and accurate observations and recordings, and pursue, appropriately, unexpected developments. Ben and Sylvia demonstrated these skills in the field, responding flexibly and openly to the situation at hand, asking guiding questions, and observing things that were not part of the original objective.

- Field observations are an important and necessary part of any new design. This type of research often uncovers issues and opportunities that would otherwise go unnoticed by having an unbiased professional researcher observe subjects at work in their normal environment. Self-reported data (information provided by the subjects on what they feel their issues are) often leaves out key pieces of information because they are not viewed as relevant. For a good overview on the usefulness of these types of studies for design as well as a basic explanation of the techniques that can be employed, see Janette Blomberg et al.'s "Ethnographic Field Methods and Their Relation to Design," in *Participatory Design: Principles and Practices* (Lawrence Erlbaum Associates, Publishers, 1993).

- Preparing an interview tool is a key part of doing field research. An interview tool is a series of open-ended questions the researchers have prepared ahead of time to ensure they cover all of the research objectives as completely as possible. The form the questions take when in the field might vary significantly to respond to the situation or to the respondent. For example, Sylvia was able to observe the way the weapon was brought to bear but did not have insight into the particulars of the control panel. Because of this, the questions from her interview tool of "How is targeting accomplished?" and "What are the restrictions?" become the far more specific "What do all these controls do, and how do you use them?" For more tips on interviewing users on-site, see Kay Corry Aubrey's "Getting Inside Your Users' Heads: 9 Interviewing Tips," *UXMatters*, September 2, 2014, www.uxmatters.com/mt/archives/2014/09/getting-inside-your-users-heads-9-interviewing-tips.php.

- Researchers must avoid closed questions when doing discovery. Closed questions are those that can be answered with a simple yes or no. They discourage discovery of the full answer and can often mislead both the researcher and the subject as they make assumptions that may not be true. Open-ended questions, on the other hand, invite explanation and thought.

The Horror Stories

Back in the Where's the Zombie conference room, the designers continued to work through similar products and competitors.

"Hey, I'm going to keep looking into the ORKON stuff in your coffee bar. I need more caffeine to wake up. And maybe some sugar. Manisha's got a line for you guys to chase too. I'll be back in a few." Trevor stretched and strode out of the room.

Max nodded, waving awkwardly as Trevor left. He could see Manisha had started a new search on her laptop and was scrolling through some kind of message board. He moved behind her, taking a chair.

"What's this?" he asked hesitantly.

"Pro-zombie action group called Dead Rights," she said, continuing to scroll through messages on the screen. "I signed up with my watcher name a couple of years ago to keep tabs on what's going on."

"Watcher name?" he asked.

She laughed. "You know, the fake name you use to check out organizations when you don't want to get inundated with e-mails or hand out your personal details. Mine is Penelope Lane."

© Rebecca Baker and CA 2017
R. Baker, *Agile UX Storytelling*, DOI 10.1007/978-1-4842-2997-2_6

Max laughed. "Really? Penny Lane?"

Manisha smiled. "Fun, huh? I used it to sign up for this Dead Rights group. Most of the time it's just crazy idealists who believe there is a way to work together if we give the zombies a chance or religious zealots who believe that this is God's will and we should just let it happen. Sometimes, though, you get some real insight that's usable. It's a lot of sifting to find it, but yes!" She tapped the screen, excitedly. "Struck gold!"

Max stared at the message. It was a posting about the government RFP they were working on. As he read, his eyes widened in alarm. They knew a frightening level of information—more than he had, certainly. But, for this group, it was all about how to destroy the weapon, not use it. A list of potential weaknesses and exploitation points made him shiver. He looked at Manisha's grin and shook his head.

"This is terrifying," he said plainly. "How can you be excited?"

"No, this is terrific!" she said, turning to face him fully, grabbing his arm. Don't you see? This gives us an instant laundry list of all the things we have to address in our design and account for! We always have to look for edge cases, weaknesses, what-ifs—and here, they've just handed it to us on a silver platter. This makes writing the horror stories so much easier."

Max's bewilderment must've been reflected on his face. Manisha grimaced slightly, considering.

"Here, I'll show you." She got up and went to the whiteboard. "The first 'opportunity' they mention is the wiring for the overheat control. They believe it would be easy to rewire the control quickly to reverse the shutdown procedure into an extended 'on' state. That is, it's easy to mess up the switch and the indicators to make it look like you're turning the weapon off when, in fact, you're turning it up."

Max nodded, still feeling slightly sick at the thought. The post had very detailed instructions on how to sabotage or disable the weapon. He wondered how they had gotten their information. It was too detailed to be from a publically available source. Wasn't it?

Manisha continued, "We need a story so we design for that possibility. A horror story—one that brings the terrible consequences to the fore and makes them relatable. Horror stories, like all stories, follow a fairly predictable formula." She wrote on the board "Event + Circumstance = Result."

EVENT + CIRCUMSTANCE = RESULT

"In this case, our event is using the weapon." Over "Event" she added a stick figure operating a boxy weapon pointed at a zombie figure. "The circumstance is that the control has been sabotaged to overheat." Over "Circumstance" she added a sneaky-looking stick figure doing something to the weapon. "Our result is a melted weapon." She drew the first stick figure again with a melted boxy weapon and the zombie getting closer.

She turned back to Max. "Do you see? Do you see the story?"

Max looked at the cartoon on the board, skeptical. "But it's not a story; it's just a cartoon."

Manisha slammed her hand flat on the table, making him jump. "It *is* a story! Stories aren't all words and pages—sometimes they are pictures or songs or cartoons or poems. You use whatever form gets the point across to the most people in the most visceral way." She gestured at the wall. "Do you see what you would need to do in the product to prevent this result? The point of horror stories is to find a way to change the result."

"Well, I mean, we could improve security," Max said slowly.

"OK, good, but let's think about what we could do with the weapon and the design of the targeting software. We don't have control over the security arrangements," Manisha said, writing "Solutions" on the board.

"But we haven't designed the software yet!" Max protested.

Manisha rolled her eyes, clearly irritated at the excuse. "That's what we're doing now. We are creating a requirement for our design, a needed part of the solution, based off of the story we just discovered."

"You said 'discovered' but you wrote that story." Max was feeling desperate. This was not how you did things. She was pulling things out of thin air. People would die if they weren't careful and certain of everything.

"Max," she said with a sigh. "I did discover this story when I read that post on the Dead Rights board. All of the elements were there. I just put them into a story form—a cartoon. I did not make it up. This is a real possibility that real people are contemplating."

She walked away from the board and sat down next to him. "I know this is... a lot. And it's not easy. This is not how you're used to working, is it?"

Max shook his head, thinking he was spending a lot of time shaking his head today. The thought made him smile. "Yeah, it's pretty different. I get it, as an intellectual exercise, but I don't think...no, scratch that, I don't feel like it's reality based, you know? We're just talking about made-up stories." He raised his hand as she started to protest. "And there's more than just a bad application review on the line here." He gestured at her cartoon. "People could die."

She smiled, nodding her head in understanding. "Exactly. Exactly! You're getting it! Did you think about that part before you saw this cartoon? That people could die?"

Max frowned, looking at her and then back at the board. Had he? Had he really thought about it before he saw that picture? He had been horrified when he read the post, but that was more about the fact that people were contemplating hurting other people to defend zombies, something he could barely wrap his head around. If he was honest with himself, the answer was no, he hadn't really thought about the impact of the design on the safety of the operator until Manisha drew it on the board. It was seeing the picture, the story, that had made him think of the frightening consequences of failure.

Manisha started tapping his arm excitedly. "You didn't, right? If I had written up a requirement that said something like 'must prevent tampering of ignition switch,' you wouldn't have thought of how serious the consequences of that happening would've been. And I can guarantee that everyone else on the team would've depersonalized it as well."

She jumped up, going back to the board and tapping on the picture of the looming zombie. "This makes it tangible. It makes it personal. It makes it *real*. It's our job, our mission, to turn this horror story into something else. We need to rewrite the ending."

"Do we have the opportunity to alter the hardware configuration? Introduce feedback opportunities for the software?" Max asked.

"Yes. Part of our work will be partnering with the inventors, if we win the contract. Hardware alterations are definitely in scope."

"In that case, I would introduce a feedback loop for every primary control in the weapon that would let us run a test on those controls individually to ensure they are working as intended. Or," he said, starting to get excited as he thought about the problem, "we could create a thumbprint lock for the weapon to access any of the electronics inside. The hardware group could look at ways to insert an emergency shutdown in case of overheating— something purely mechanical so it couldn't be bypassed."

Manisha hurriedly scribbled his ideas under solutions.

"Let's do a map to look for opportunities." Manisha quickly drew a map on the board, showing the weapon in storage, being prepped for operation, in operation, being transported between areas, and back in storage.

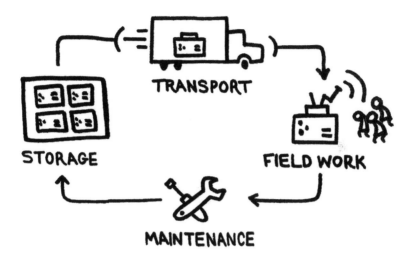

She inserted the sneaky stick figure in the storage area with the caption "Tampering in Storage."

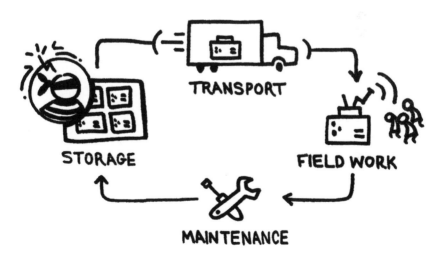

She stepped back looking at it. "Where else could the tampering occur?"

"Well, it depends. Is there a wireless interface for any part of this?"

Manisha shook her head. "No, it's all wired."

"Then I think that's probably it for the hardware tampering. But there's still software. We could get hacked in storage too, if they get access. We'll need to account for that. Most of the stuff we do now doesn't have to be secured. This is different."

Manisha nodded her head. "Good point, we'll need to add that to our alternates for this problem." She started writing it on the board.

The conference room door opened, and Trevor walked in.

"Trev, where have you been?" Manisha asked.

"Peace out, boss, I brought sustenance!" he announced, waving a white paper box at them. "Did you know that this place is connected to the underground food court? And did you know that they have a *donut* shop there?" He said *donut* with a hushed reverence that made Max laugh.

Manisha rolled her eyes. "Trevor has a thing for donuts," she said with amusement. "Bring them over here—I could do with a little boost."

They dug into the donuts, working through the other posts from the Dead Rights board that talked about specific sabotage opportunities. Trevor had dug up more on the ORKON targeting systems. They were very glitzy, and the virtual reality aspect was incredibly compelling. But he'd found feedback from field tests that indicated they were missing a big piece by shutting out the environment to such an extreme degree. Trevor thought they might try to make a play for an augmented reality interface, which would certainly look slick.

"But," he said through a mouthful of pink sprinkles, "the academic research I've found suggests that for targeting multiple subjects in sequence, AR is just a distraction. People are just too distractible to be able to make good targeting decisions en masse."

Manisha considered this. "That would imply a completely automated targeting system would work better."

Trevor and Max both started talking at once.

"Yes! That would do it! We could use the mass system tracking to…"

"That's right! We could speed up the individual targeting mechanism…."

Soon they were all at the board, as the requirements list grew longer. Sketches of horror stories and opportunity maps covered the surface.

Max didn't know how long they'd been there when his phone started ringing. He pulled it out of his pocket, glancing at the name. It was Sylvia. She must be calling from the base. He answered quickly, hoping she had some good insights to share.

"Hey Sylvia! What's—" the words died on his tongue as she interrupted him talking quickly. Manisha and Trevor looked at him, growing more concerned as they watched his face grow more ashen.

"Oh crap, we'll be right there…," he trailed off as she interrupted again.

"Yeah, OK. Call me as soon as you get out. Just tell us what you need. We'll do it." A few more words. "Ok, you got it. I'll let them know. Take care of yourself. And call me in an hour, OK?"

Max hung up and turned to the other two. They looked at him expectantly.

"There's been an explosion."

Key Takeaways

- Understanding the difficult, nonideal circumstances is important when gathering requirements and use cases. Your solution must be able to operate in all kinds of tricky situations to be effective. A great example of this is designing solutions for mobile devices. Many designers approach mobile design as a smaller version of the desktop software. Unfortunately, by their very nature, mobile devices change the context of use by being unpredictable in their environment. A mobile device could (and is often) used outside during a baseball game, while waiting in line at the grocery store or bank, or while lying down in bed in the dark. This change in context from the office to the field can mean a significant change in how the product is used, what workflows are important, and how accessible the software is. Uncovering stories about how the product could be used outside the happy path is critical to ensure the solution accounts for and addresses those situations. From a solution standpoint, it may mean including an emergency shutdown switch or simply thinking through the error messages that need to appear.

- Because different people have different communication styles, different people respond to different levels of formality in their stories. Similar to the challenges with use cases, stories must walk the line of having too many or too few details, failing to take into account both the users and the stakeholders. Creating and using stories effectively is part art and part science. For a history of use case creation and the challenges encountered with the various methodologies used, see Alistair Cockburn's "Use Cases, Ten Years Later," `http://alistair.cockburn.us/Use+cases,+ten+years+later`.

- Storytelling is often more effective through pictures than words—providing simple illustrations can get an idea across more quickly than long descriptions. Cartoonists such as Liza Donnelly (`www.huffingtonpost.com/vala-afshar/the-art-of-storytelling_b_7827738.html`) understand the power of stories and use them regularly. For more insight into storytelling through cartoons, see Scott McCloud's *Understanding Comics: The Invisible Art* (William Morrow Paperbacks, 1994).

- Journey maps are frequently used to provide an overview of an entire experience, not just a single workflow. These maps include all of the relevant decision points and touch points during a user's experience. Maps can also be focused on a single narrative or story to visualize parts of that story that might not otherwise be obvious. You can use journey maps to identify potential problem areas, such as the potential for tampering with the switch on your zombie-killing gun, or to identify opportunities for your software to fill gaps in the customer experience, such as adding alerts to your ticketing app to let the customer know of updates while they are en route to an event. To read more about journey mapping, check out `https://www.smashingmagazine.com/2015/01/all-about-customer-journey-mapping/`.

The Wreckage

Sylvia blinked, confused, as she woke up in a world of smoke and pain. She was lying on her back near the jeep. Her head throbbed, and her skin felt burned in several places. She tried to push herself up, but nausea quickly made her stop. Turning her head to the right, she could see Ben lying in a heap an arm's length away. His clothes were smoking in spots, blood was running down his face, and he wasn't moving. Rolling onto her side, she tried again to rise with the idea of checking on him but started to heave immediately. A sharp, stabbing pain ricocheted through her brain, as she emptied her stomach on the ground. She could vaguely hear muffled shouts that seemed to come from a long way off, but the roaring in her head drowned out all but her immediate misery. Blearily, she tried to look toward Ben and was shocked to see a zombie, not 5 feet from his prone form. It had once been a short woman; a "have a nice day" button was still stuck on the remains of her shirt, and the bright yellow smiley face was incongruous on the filthy rags. It moved slowly toward the unconscious researcher. Without thinking, Sylvia grabbed a rock and flung it weakly at the shuffling form.

"Go away!" she croaked. "Get away from him!"

The rock bounced near the zombie's feet. It stopped, looking first at the stone and then back at Sylvia, crouched on her knees. She held her breath. It looked at her, and the eyes…the eyes weren't the dead eyes of zombies on the news reports. They were alive, and they saw her—really saw her. It smiled, a horrible hungry smile. Her breath caught, and she started sobbing in panic as it started shuffling toward her, ignoring Ben.

Suddenly a crack rang out, and the zombie toppled forward, boneless and truly dead. Behind it, Sergeant Caldwell stood, calmly pointing his pistol at the

© Rebecca Baker and CA 2017
R. Baker, *Agile UX Storytelling*, DOI 10.1007/978-1-4842-2997-2_7

zombie. He emptied three more shots into the head and then strode over to Ben. He looked up at Sylvia.

"He's OK." His voice seemed to be coming from a long way away. She started crying again as he came over to her, helping her to her feet. She clung to him, not caring that she was hurt, filthy, and smelled of sick, only that she was alive.

"Hey, you're OK too," Caldwell said gently. "Just breathe. Medics will be here in a minute."

The next hour was a whirlwind of activity and questions. Medics arrived, bundling Ben onto a gurney and rushing him to the base hospital. They wanted to take her as well, but a security detail arrived at the same time and would not let her leave without questions. There was a brief argument during which she made out the words *concussion* and *witness*, but it was difficult to hear with the constant ringing in her ears. In the end, the medic, a young dark-haired man named Joe, lost. He treated her cuts and burns, wrapping her in a blanket, and then stood nearby, glaring and tapping his foot impatiently. Sergeant Thomas from the security detail ignored Joe and put on what she imagined he meant to be a gentle smile for her. Unfortunately, the smile reminded her all too much of the zombie, and she started shaking uncontrollably. Joe quickly swooped in, putting an arm around her and giving Sergeant Thomas a pointed look. The sergeant sighed.

"Ma'am," he started, speaking slowly and softly. "Can you tell me what happened here?"

"We were walking back to the j-j-jeep when there was a big noise, and I was being pushed forward. I think I banged my head. Then there was a zombie that tried to...that tried to...." Tears started streaming down her face. She couldn't seem to force out the words "tried to eat Ben." The sergeant nodded, understandingly.

"It's OK, ma'am. You're safe now. Did you hear or see anything before the big noise?"

Sylvia tried to think back. "Maybe. I think there was kind of a whining noise, really high-pitched, just before everything went crazy. I remember wondering what that was." She looked over to the fence where the weapon had been. It was gone, a smoking hole where it had once stood. The section of fence it had been next to was mangled, blown over. There were no zombies in evidence. Sylvia wondered what happened to the crew working on the weapon. And what had happened to the zombies? Sylvia's eyes grew wide as she started to panic, looking around to make sure there were none nearby.

"Ma'am, it's OK. All of the zombies were eliminated. The one Caldwell took out was the last one. We've accounted for all of them."

The sergeant continued to question her, asking her the same question different ways, gently teasing more information from her rattled brain. *He'd make a good researcher*, she thought, as she leaned against Joe. He seemed willing to hold her while she talked to the sergeant, and she appreciated the support. Every time she started to cry again, he gave her a little hug, and it helped her get on top of it. Finally, after what seemed like hours, the sergeant closed his notebook, thanking her politely for her cooperation. Joe helped her get up and guided her to a waiting ambulance.

"Oh! I just realized—I better call Max and let him know what happened." She pulled her cell phone out, hitting the speed dial for Max. He answered on the second ring.

"Max! I don't want you to get upset, but Ben and I have been in kind of an accident. There was an explosion….no, no don't come down here, they won't let you in anyway. The whole base is locked down." She glanced at Joe who nodded affirmation. "Ben got knocked out and is in the base hospital, and I'm headed there next. They said he's OK, but I'll let you know more when I find out more. I think it was the weapon that exploded…. Yeah, OK, I'll call you back in a bit." She hung up and gingerly climbed into the ambulance.

Joe sat in the back with her as they rolled toward the hospital.

"So," he said. "What brought you out here today?"

"You mean I don't look like military to you?" she asked with a wry grin, gesturing to her slightly burnt neon yellow jacket, black T-shirt with "I believe" in acid green letters, and black jeans.

He laughed and she continued, "I'm a user researcher. You know what that is?" he shook his head. "It's my job to figure out how people use things, to find out where they are having problems, and to help people who design things to figure out how to solve those problems."

"Cool job!" Joe said. "So, what are you researching out here?"

"Some kind of anti-zombie weapon. I think that's what exploded, but…I don't know how or why."

"Well, I guess it's a good thing you're a researcher then," Joe said, winking. The ambulance had stopped, and he leaned over to open the doors and hop out. "Because you'll be able to find out!"

Sylvia knew he was joking, trying to keep her mind off the terrible things that had just happened. But, in her mind, she had already started to break down the possible causes of the explosion and catalog the things she'd seen. She needed to talk to Ben to compare notes and see what she might've missed. Preoccupied, she let herself be put into a wheelchair and rolled into the hospital.

Subsequent examinations revealed that Joe was right—she had a mild concussion, as well as multiple contusions, burns, and a sprained shoulder. She was told that she had been lucky. She had been far enough away from the explosion that her injuries had been relatively minor. Ben had cracked his head on a rock when he'd been thrown and needed stitches. He also had whiplash, contusions, and a broken arm. He was awake and sitting up when they finally wheeled her in to see him. He looked subdued, serious.

"Hey," he said quietly. "Are you OK?"

"Yeah, I'm OK." Sylvia ran a hand through her hair. "I stink, and I'm sore, and I want a shower, but I'm OK. You?"

He chuckled a bit. "I'm OK too. Just shook up, you know? I don't remember anything about what happened. One minute I'm walking up a hill, and the next I'm here."

Sylvia filled him in on everything that had happened.

"So, we think the weapon exploded then. Did you note how badly the fence was damaged?" Sylvia was grateful when Ben jumped on the problem immediately, glossing over the near-death encounter. She didn't think she could talk about that without getting the shakes again.

"Yes. A section of 30 feet or so was blown over and twisted." She frowned. "Come to think of it, it seemed like the damage on the fence side was much worse than the damage on our side. The explosion must have been directed that way…assuming it was the weapon that exploded and not something else. Did you see which way it was pointed before you started walking up the hill?"

"They'd just managed to wrestle it around so that it was pointing away from the fence and were wrangling toward the truck." Ben paused, thinking. "Assuming we're right, that would imply the explosion was directed outward from the control panel, not from the muzzle of the weapon. What are you thinking? Equipment malfunction? The controls seemed pretty jenky."

Sylvia nodded. "Malfunction, overheating, something like that. The control panel was the least reinforced piece. I remember thinking that when we talk to the inventors, we should see about getting some modifications. It looked like the panel could be easily removed, unlike the rest of the thing." She chewed on her lip, thinking. "The technician was kind of clueless about a lot of the dials on the thing—strictly a "turn this, point it there, push this button" kind of operation. No training in what was actually happening under the covers. Were any of the folks you talked to more savvy on the internal workings?"

Ben shook his head, wincing and rubbing his neck with his good hand. "No. And they were all pretty skeptical about its usefulness. According to Karen, the squad leader, they had been given this whole thing with very little notice or instruction. She used the phrase…," he trailed off as he started searching for his notebook. Sylvia found it in a bag nearby with his phone and shattered tablet. He flipped quickly through the pages. "Here it is! She said they were given an 'alpha charlie' when they asked for training."

Sylvia was surprised. "They got chewed out for requesting training? That's unusual."

As they spoke, Caldwell appeared in the doorway, looking slightly singed and battered but none the worse for wear. He didn't smile but regarded them both seriously.

"We have investigators looking into the cause of the explosion, but based on initial data, it looks like the weapon was tampered with. It's unclear whether an incendiary device was planted on the weapon or if the weapon itself was compromised." He straightened his throat. "I understand that you both are under a nondisclosure agreement as part of your work here. I must remind you that this extends to today's incident."

"Of course," Sylvia said nodding. She knew she should be thinking about a way to get the information to the team, but her head still felt fuzzy, and she hurt all over. "We won't talk to anyone outside our company. Can we," she started hesitantly, trying to find the right words, "can we talk to some of your team later? You know, after we all get out of here."

Ben nodded his agreement gingerly, adding, "Also, would it be possible for us to talk to the inventors and share what we saw today? Not the explosion but, you know, the way it was used. Maybe we can find some way to get around the, um, awkwardness of field use."

Caldwell smiled at that. "Yeah, the thing is a bugger to use, no argument there. I'll see what I can do for you. I can't promise anything—outside my pay grade— but what you're asking for makes sense. But with regard to the explosion, I'd appreciate you keeping your observations to yourselves. Now, if you'll excuse me, I need to check on my team." He turned sharply on his heel and strode down the hall.

Sylvia turned back to Ben as Caldwell's steps faded down the hall. "We've got to talk to those inventors. The thing is unusable in its current state, no matter what genius we come up with from a software standpoint."

"I agree. There's a ton of things we need to account for that just weren't in the RFP. We'll need to make adjustments to the stories and characters accordingly." Ben groaned as he settled back into the bed. "But, not right now. Right now, I just want to rest."

"Yeah, well, I hope you don't snore. They told me I'm rooming with you tonight," Sylvia countered.

"Alright, tomorrow morning we can gather our notes and then give them a call. I wonder how long we have to stay here."

Ben shrugged. "No idea. I suspect at least until Caldwell has heard back from whomever he reports to."

They talked for a bit longer, but neither felt up to much. The nurse returned and helped Sylvia settle in the other bed in the room. As the lights went out, she wondered if she snored.

Key Takeaways

- Field research lets you see the problems in the situation. The users who are involved with the process may accept the situation as immutable; outside observers can question whether the awkward process that is being followed is really necessary.

- Often research work involves signing a nondisclosure agreement. When a company is showing its product to a user for testing purposes, the user signs the agreements. However, when researchers are observing a new system for the purposes of a bid, they will sign the agreement. A nondisclosure agreement prohibits sharing confidential information about the system with outside parties.

The Balance

Max grimaced as he got off the phone, turning to Manisha.

"Something exploded during the demo. Sylvia says Ben was taken to the hospital. They've been questioning her. She was kind of incoherent, and I think she was having a hard time hearing me."

Manisha looked pale, shaken at the news. "We should go to them! Go get them and bring them back!" she grabbed her messenger bag and started stuffing her laptop and other papers back into it. Trevor was already on his feet and moving toward the door.

"Wait! No, we can't." Max caught him by the arm. "They won't let anyone on the base right now. Sylvia said she'd call us back when we could come get her or when she knew more. We have to wait," he added miserably.

"Wait? *Wait?* No." Manisha pulled her laptop back out of her bag and snapped it open. "We don't 'wait.' Waiting is passive. We plan, we dig, we investigate, we *act!*" Her voice became louder, growing in passion and resonance. "We do *not* wait."

Max was amazed at her reaction. Yes, the news had been shocking, horrible. Trevor shook his head, clearly stunned at the turn in events. Max knew how he felt. He was a software designer. Sylvia was a user researcher. They didn't... get exploded. They got carpal tunnel syndrome and high blood pressure. But still, he looked at Manisha and realized he didn't really know her at all.

© Rebecca Baker and CA 2017

R. Baker, *Agile UX Storytelling*, DOI 10.1007/978-1-4842-2997-2_8

Trevor looked over at Manisha and then back at Max, raising his eyebrows. Max glanced at the storyteller. She was reading through some text on her screen. She found what she needed and pulled out her cell phone, dialing quickly. Max looked back at Trevor, who shrugged. Manisha saw them looking at her and waved her hand dismissively at them, turning away.

"Let's go get some coffee," he said quietly. Max nodded and followed him out of the room. As he closed the door behind him, he heard Manisha say, "Colonel Peterson, please."

Trevor let out a long breath as they walked toward the break room. "Crazy, man. Just crazy. First the zombie in the building and now this. If I was paranoid, I'd swear it was a conspiracy." He kept walking past the break room toward the elevator to the underground. Max trailed along with him, still processing.

"Fortunately," Trevor added as he punched the down button, "I'm way too laid back to be paranoid." Max smiled at the other man's attempt at levity. Too much was happening too fast. His stomach churned as he thought of Sylvia and Ben at the hospital. The elevator dinged open, and the two designers stepped on. Trevor punched the button for the underground, and they started their smooth decent. Both men were quiet, thinking.

"So," Max said, trying to break the awkward silence. "Do you actually have any blood in your blood stream, or is it pure coffee?"

Trevor laughed. "Hey, it's a hazard of the profession! And you haven't been around Manisha enough to understand that she is always 'on.' That woman is nonstop."

Max glanced over at him. "Storyteller, huh?" The other man smiled, shaking his head slightly.

"Yeah, yeah, I know. Super hokey." He looked down at his feet for a minute and then up at Max, serious. "But it works, you know? We're kind of...everyone thinks they're really, really good at communicating. But that's not true. We're really, really bad at it, but because we think we're good at it, we just assume other people are stupid or, worse, that we know what they really want. I still screw up all the time, but the story templates help me get back on track. They make me think about how other people see it and how to help them see what I'm saying. It's not the solution to world hunger or anything, for sure. But it does make talking to someone else easier. And it keeps you honest about your own...filters."

The elevator doors opened onto an underground corridor. Cold air rushed to meet them, causing Max to shiver slightly. The underground had been part of downtown Dallas for as long as he could remember. But when the zombies came, it became an easily fortifiable way to connect a multitude of businesses together. While other restaurants and shops struggled to adjust to securing their storefronts, those located in the underground thrived. The two designers quickly walked down a ramp that opened into a large food court. Trevor gestured at the coffee shop, and they made their way through a milling crowd to place their orders.

Coffee in hand, they wandered over to one of the metal tables scattered around the food court. Trevor looked pensive as he sipped his cold brew.

"You know," Max started, "the automated targeting…I think it's got potential. Do you think we can get a hold of the inventors and check some things? I mean, the specifications we've got have it being really slow. Is that something we can work with?"

Trevor nodded, thoughtfully. "I'm a software guy, but I think the angle is right. With the current constraints, the system is unusable for the type of targeting the RFP has listed. The question isn't so much can we do it—it's tech, and that's about as close to magic as you can get—it's whether it's cost-effective. One thing our product manager has pounded into our heads is cost. Everything is possible if you have unlimited resources."

"Tell me about it. Justin is all about 'cost' and 'marketability.' He's a total killjoy sometimes. He never gets excited about improving the usability of something. I mean, we've got some seriously clunky workflows that I'd love to overhaul! But if it's not going to sell more product, he doesn't care." Max stopped and corrected himself. "That's not entirely true. He does care. It just doesn't make a difference when he's putting in his vote on what we spend time on."

Trevor shrugged sympathetically. "Yeah, same with us. But I get it. Making products, it's a balancing act, y'know? You could make the coolest thing in the world, but if no one wants to buy it, well…," he paused, fishing out a pen from his pocket. He started drawing a Venn diagram on a napkin. "You've got to have three things for a product to be successful. It's got to be usable—that's us. It's got to be possible—that's development. And it's got to be salable—that's product. If you have only one or two, the product is worthless. For example, if it's possible and usable, you still can't sell it. If it's salable and possible, you can't use it. And if it's salable and usable, it may be impossible."

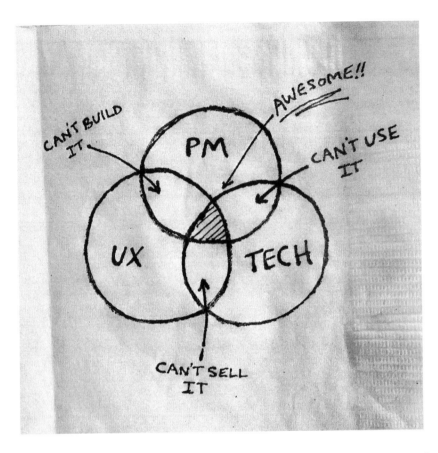

"Of course," he said looking at the sketch. "There's a million other pieces that come together too. But the idea is you can't just concentrate on your own little world. You've got to make sure you're part of the whole team."

Max studied the napkin. It made sense. He remembered a product he'd conspired to make with Owen, their lead developer, on the side. A mobile app that let you message your friends when you spotted a zombie. He and Owen were convinced they had the new market disrupter and worked weekends and after hours to make a prototype. It was beautiful, elegant, efficient—everything they wanted it to be. They brought it to Justin, full of righteous pride in their baby. And he proceeded to tear it to pieces from a market perspective. They'd been unaware there were other apps on the market that did precisely what they were proposing—and had been for at least a year. And that those apps were doing poorly because the social media giants already had plug-ins to capture this particular use case. Also, they hadn't thought past the initial release. What would come next? How would they expand the market once they had captured it? The following lecture on pricing structure still left Max with a headache. It had been an unpleasant lesson in the need for market research and understanding.

"You're right," Max sighed. "We need to pull in Justin, as the product manager, on this as well as Owen, as the lead developer, and see what kind of cost we're looking at. But," he paused, sipping his latte, "it may not matter. The automatic targeting problem is a big one, and the largest issue is the hardware. If we can't make that more agile, the software won't matter."

"I agree." Trevor said. "We need to keep an open mind, though. We can't let the stories take over."

Max sat back, surprised. "Wait, I thought you were all about the stories! What's this—second thoughts?"

Trevor chuckled, "Nah, you know it's just that anything good can be bad too, right? Take the stories we've made so far. They work because they're based on requirements, use cases, things we've drawn out of the RFP, or our secondary research. And what have they gotten us so far?" he paused as Max shrugged. "Not much. They're a start, not much more. They're keeping us all on the same page. They're sparking some ideas. They're helping us figure out the questions we need to ask so we can go find out more. But they're not solving the problem. And they won't. It's like…," he, paused, searching for words, "stories are great because they help you communicate your ideas. And that's super important, right? But the thing is, when you tell a story, you're communicating *your* idea in a way that is easy to understand and easy to latch on to. But, maybe you aren't telling the whole story. Maybe you only told the part that makes me want to believe in what you believe. When we create stories without data and without multiple perspectives, we stop being able to think logically about things. It's like that balancing act between dev, product, and design we talked about earlier." He pulled out his pen and started drawing another sketch.

"See, the more solution-oriented a story is," he said as he drew a graph, showing "Solution" on the y-axis, "the more likely we are to believe it, without checking our facts." He labeled the x-axis "Belief." He continued, "The problem is that the actual facts lie somewhere closer to the beginning."

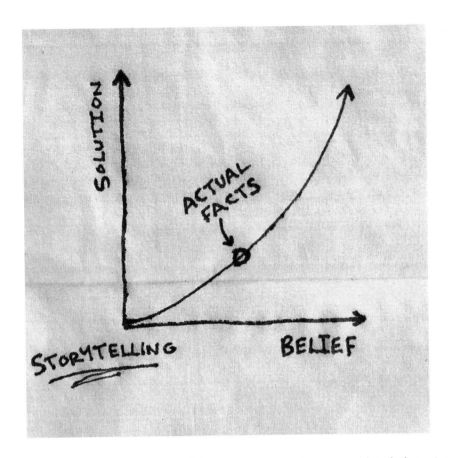

"As a result, we have to be careful to not tell ourselves super-detailed stories about the solution until we get all the facts. Solution stories are the most seductive ones, since our brains naturally want resolution."

"But," Max protested, "what about the story Manisha told? And the horror stories we wrote? Aren't we likely to do the same thing with those?"

Trevor shook his head. "It's always a risk—like, we could make a horror story so visceral that we lose track of the fact that it's unlikely to happen and is just an edge case. And that happened to us a lot when we first started using stories, so it's a good thing to be on the lookout for. But," he tapped the napkin for emphasis, "solutions are always a trouble spot. We love a good puzzle because we love finding the solution. Once we find one, it's hard for us to let go and see other possibilities. Also, you start to try to make the facts fit your solution instead of the other way around."

"Hmmm...." Max thought about it.

"Honestly, I love the automated targeting idea, and I feel like it's the right answer. But we know too little, and I'm afraid if we go too far down that road, we'll be unable to respond if something comes up that makes the solution untenable. It's too early to lock anything down, especially without the field observations." He paused awkwardly, clearly thinking about the researchers, and then muttered, "They've got to be…I mean, I'm sure they're OK."

Max could see the frustration and helplessness on the other man's face. He felt it too. He thought of Sylvia and Ben—what must they be thinking right now? They were probably totally freaked out. He wondered if Justin hadn't been right. Maybe there *was* something going on. He told Trevor what the product manager had said after the zombie scare in the office.

"Conspiracy?" his laugh seemed forced. "I told you, I'm too laid back for that kind of stuff. It takes energy, y'know—being paranoid and all." Max could see the other man's hands tremble he took another sip of his cold brew and glanced behind him. "Let's get back upstairs. Manisha is probably finished rallying whatever troops she was going to rally by now."

Max stood, trailing the other designer out of the food court and toward the elevators. He couldn't help thinking about what an odd reaction Trevor had had to the conspiracy theory idea. It was like even thinking about it made him uncomfortable. He shrugged as they stepped onto the elevator and headed back to the office.

Key Takeaways

- Good software is a balancing act between all participants, ensuring that competing motivations—efficiency, usability, and profitability—are all taken into account.

- Stories have been shown repeatedly to be an effective communication tool when conveying unfamiliar or difficult subject matter. For an interesting review of the arguments for and against using narratives to convey fact-based information, see Michael Dahlstrom's "Using narratives and storytelling to communicate science with nonexpert audiences," Proceeding of the National Academy of Sciences in the United States (2014), www.pnas.org/content/111/Supplement_4/13614.full.

- Good stories can skip the logical part of your brain and go straight for the emotional center. For this reason, it's important to make sure you have all the facts, or at least as many as you can reasonably gather, prior to making your solution story. For more information on the dark side of stories, see Jonathan Gottschall's "Theranos and the Dark Side of Storytelling," Harvard Business Review, October 2016, https://hbr.org/2016/10/theranos-and-the-dark-side-of-storytelling.

Problems

The sound of a keyboard being abused met Max and Trevor when they returned to the conference room. Manisha glanced up as they walked in.

"Oh good, you're back!" she said. "I called our contact for the RFP—in light of what happened at today's demo, they've agreed to give us access to the inventors. Of course, all the applicants will have the same opportunity, so we'll need to keep that in mind. I'd really like to send Ben and Sylvia out, but I'm not sure if they'll be up to it after the explosion."

Max nodded. He was surprised how quickly she'd been able to get the government to agree to the interview. "They'll call us. Then they can decide if they can go out or if a couple of us can do it. What's the time frame for the interview?"

"Three days from now."

Trevor whistled. "Whoa, that's quick! What did you say to them?"

Manisha grinned. "I just pointed out the obvious—that with no prototype to demo or work with, the timeline for the proposals would need to be extended significantly. Nobody wants that."

Max looked at her confused. "Wait. Why not? I mean why do they care? It's not like there's an immediate need for this thing. Right?"

Manisha shook her head. "Not that I'm aware of, although I will say there's a lot more energy and urgency around this RFP than the ones I've dealt with before. No, I suspect it has more to do with the timing from a budgeting standpoint. They want this awarded before an end-of-year review. Any significant delay pushes the award into next year."

© Rebecca Baker and CA 2017
R. Baker, *Agile UX Storytelling*, DOI 10.1007/978-1-4842-2997-2_9

After some short good-byes, Manisha and Trevor started packing up to head home. Max noticed his cell phone was down to 20 percent battery and had just started looking for his adapter when Justin walked in.

An uncomfortable silence crept across the room. The product manager stood there, looking awkward and embarrassed for a moment before blurting out, "Look, I'm sorry guys. I don't know what my problem was, but I know it was my problem, not yours." He took a deep breath and looked directly at Manisha, who regarded him solemnly. "I apologize. In the future, I'll try not to let my emotional baggage intrude on work."

Manisha cocked her head to one side and gave him a slight smile. "Of course. We all have our demons."

Justin looked surprised for a moment before he recovered himself and turned to Max.

"Hey, would you have time for a drink?" He gestured to his watch. "It's, you know, after 6, so…."

"A drink sounds awesome, Justin." Max smiled at his friend. He was exhausted, but it would be good to hang out and decompress a bit.

Manisha rose and started packing her laptop bag. Trevor followed suit.

"It's been quite a day," she said, still smiling slightly. "9 a.m. tomorrow?"

"You bet," Max agreed. He turned to Justin. "Let's go."

They walked out of the conference room, leaving Manish and Trevor to pack up and find their way out.

"The Hollow Tree?" Max asked. Justin nodded, avoiding meeting his friend's eyes. They walked in awkward silence to the elevators. As the doors slid open, Max realized his friend probably didn't know about the explosion yet. He glanced at Justin and realized just how ragged he looked. Deciding to wait until they were sitting down to tell him about Sylvia and Ben, he searched for something to say.

"So…," he started as the doors closed behind them, "is this going to be another one of those special little snowflake projects, or do you think you can sell this beastie when it's done?"

Justin snorted. Max knew he prided himself on the ability to sell anything but that he despised being pigeon-holed into doing custom work for individual clients—"special little snowflakes" he called them. A smile crept onto Justin's lips as he continued to look down at this feet.

"I can see a potential market. I just started doing the due diligence today. Fortunately, it's mostly reading—the new team has done a decent work-up already. I just wish Angie had looped me in earlier. It seems like all the Virtual Zombie folks have known about this for a while…." He trailed off as the doors slid open onto the underground.

The Hollow Tree squatted at the center of the underground, an odd pub with a fake tree trunk in the center that was circled by a polished bar. The décor, with dark wood, several dart boards, and tall booths with worn black leather upholstery arranged like spokes around the bar, was eclectic to say the least. A couple of overstuffed chairs lurked in the corner, looking enticingly comfy. You could always tell folks who were new to the pub because they would be lured in by those chairs, both of which hid devilishly uncomfortable springs that managed to poke you in exactly the wrong places no matter how you sat in them. They were empty now, except for a backpack someone had laid on one to keep it out of the way during their dart game.

Justin and Max slid into their favorite booth near the deceptive chairs. Becky, the bartender, raised an eyebrow at them. Max nodded. A minute later, she set two Ugly Pugs on their table.

"Tab?" she queried.

"Yep. And two burgers please," Max replied, handing her his card. She nodded, taking the card and striding back to the bar. Max and Justin had been coming to the Hollow Tree for more than a year now, and Becky knew their order by heart. Max tried to think if he'd ever heard her utter more than one word at a time and couldn't. Her no-nonsense demeanor was as comforting to the clientele as the leather booths—there were no expectations of chatting about your day, flirting, or indeed anything except the excellent local beer, burgers, and fries. Low-key classical music played over the speakers, quiet enough to enable easy conversation.

The men clinked their beers then took a drink. Max sighed.

"I need to catch you up on today's research visit." He quickly recapped the day's events.

Justin just stared at Max, his mouth hanging open.

"Explosion?" he said blankly. "They…they got exploded?"

Max laughed nervously. "Well, that's a weird way to put it, but yeah, they um, something exploded. They're mostly OK, but that guy Ben has a broken arm and—"

Justin interrupted him. "And *when* did this happen exactly?" He took a long pull on his beer.

Max shook his head. "I know how it sounds. I mean," he paused, thinking. "It's pretty freaky. What are the odds?"

"Exactly. What are the odds?" Justin looked solemnly at him. "There is something going on here. Something…bad. I'm a product manager, not some kind of…," he gestured with his beer, "I don't know, adventure hero. This is scary, and I don't like it. I'd like to write it off as just a coincidence, but I can't."

"But, I mean, seriously—why would anyone want to sabotage us? Or this project? It doesn't make any sense," Max protested.

Justin shook his head. "That's just your comfort zone talking." He took another drink. "You don't want it to be a problem, so you're trying to see all the ways it's not a problem. I get it. I want it not to be something bad too. But wanting it to be a coincidence is not the same thing as being objective and recognizing that there is a threat. And there is a threat. I can't bury my head in the sand and ignore it, and I won't let you do it either."

Max shifted uncomfortably. Justin had a point. Trevor's reaction to the idea of a conspiracy had been so strange. Something was up—he just didn't want something to be up. He wanted everything to be the way it had been before he came to work this morning. His thoughts were interrupted as Becky strode up to their table, a plate in each hand. The enticing smell of a perfectly cooked burger made Max's mouth water as she slid the plate with an enormous cheeseburger and mountain of parmesan fries in front of him. She nodded at the beers the men held and arched an eyebrow. Both men nodded.

"Yeah, a refill would be great, thanks," Justin said.

Becky nodded and strode back to the bar without a word.

Justin looked down at his burger with a wry smile. "Well, at least some things are still just as good as they've always been. I'm starving!"

Max and Justin dug in to their food, savoring the juicy, well-seasoned burgers and crisp fries. The ketchup was something Becky made herself and tasted like Max imagined real ketchup was meant to taste—sweet and salty with a hint of some kind of spice that complemented the parmesan fries perfectly. There were many great places to eat in and around Dallas, but his favorite was always this—a cheeseburger and fries at the Hollow Tree.

The two men ate in companionable silence, giving the food the attention it deserved. Once the last bite of the last fry had been consumed, Becky appeared, and the plates disappeared, almost in the same moment. Max leaned back and smiled. Between the slight buzz from the beer and the post-burger glow, he was able to relax and really think about things objectively, without the stress and fear that had chased him all day.

"You're right," he told Justin. He watched his friend take another drink from his beer and nod.

"Good. I'm glad you decided to listen and not try to be some kind of Polly Anna."

Max shook his head. "Not so fast. I agree that something is up, but that's a long way from a conspiracy."

Justin rolled his eyes. "Whatever. As long as you're listening and not just shutting me out." He paused, rummaging around in his pockets. He pulled out a beat-up black notebook and cheap ballpoint pen. As he opened it, Max could see dark scribbles covering the pages.

"As I see it, we've got the following events of note." He swiveled the notebook around so Max could see his cramped writing. "One—we buy a new company as a strategic play for a government contract. This move is kept a secret from most of the people in our company."

"Not that this is particularly strange," Max interjected.

Justin waived a hand irritably at him. "I'm not saying it is; just let me get through this. Two—during the official onboarding, we have a zombie-in-the-building incident. The zombie is spotted but not captured or eliminated."

"Wait, you mean they didn't find or kill it?" Max felt suddenly cold. "I mean— it's not like they can hide or be sneaky or...," he trailed off thinking about the zombie he'd seen run that morning.

"Right. More weirdness right? Three," he started writing as he spoke, "sabotage at the demo."

"Explosion," Max corrected.

Justin cocked an eyebrow at him. "Really? You think it just magically exploded while our researchers were there? Really?"

Max shook his head. "Events, not interpretations—let's look at it as objectively as we can."

Justin sighed and crossed out "sabotage" and wrote "explosion" in its place. "Fine. Then we've got all these new people running around the office that seem to know way more than they should and have connections a normal person doesn't."

Max frowned. "Who do you mean?"

"Well, your new girlfriend for one," Justin said. "I did a little checking on her while you guys were cozying up over your laptops and found some interesting things. And by 'interesting' I mean 'suspicious.'"

Max nodded cautiously, taking another pull on his beer while trying to squash the defensiveness he felt. "Go on."

"Her advisor at university is a well-known zombie sympathizer, and she's published a number of papers with him on studying zombies for a cure. And before she worked with Virtual Zombie, she and Trevor worked at StillHuman." He paused dramatically.

"StillHuman?" Max wracked his brain trying to think of where he'd heard that name. It seemed familiar.

"You know! The company that helps people whose family members have become deaders to get them contained! She's a deader sympathizer! And I bet Trevor is right there with her. They're probably the ones sabotaging this project!"

Suddenly Becky was standing at their table, hands on her hips and eyebrow raised as her eyes bore into Trevor. He looked down at his beer, suddenly subdued. "Sorry, I'll keep it down."

She nodded and looked at Max, cocking her head at his beer. "Yeah, one more round for us; then we'd better head out."

She left, and Max turned to Justin. "OK, so in college she was a deader sympathizer or at least hung out with them. How long has it been since she worked for StillHuman. It's not like a lot of folks weren't part of that movement in the early years."

Justin sighed, "Six years. But still, the zombie thing has only been going on for ten, so that's almost yesterday, you know?"

It was Max's turn to raise an eyebrow. Justin looked down at his notebook, avoiding his gaze. "I admit, it's a little thin. My sister was a deader sympathizer in college too. We lived out in Euless where there weren't any attacks or risings or anything. When she went to University of North Texas, it was all protests and rights marches and stuff. But that doesn't change the fact that we're working with someone who has ties to those kinds of people. Maybe she's not actively working against us, but maybe she is."

Max shook his head, starting to get tired. "You're seeing things that just aren't there, Jus. I mean, I get the weird coincidences with the deader break-in and the explosion. But I think this thing about Manisha and Trevor—you're reaching. You're starting to sound like one of those conspiracy theorists with the tinfoil hats."

Justin shrugged, refusing to look at him. "Maybe. Maybe not."

Max sighed. "Look, let's take a step back and try to take the emotion and paranoia out of it, OK?"

Justin looked up at him, suspiciously. "You think I'm paranoid?"

"Maybe a little. Let's talk about the work and see if we can catch up with where everyone else is. That should give us real things to focus on, not just suppositions and rumors."

Justin rolled his bottle between his hands, thoughtfully. "OK. I'm not saying there's *not* a conspiracy going on, but I have been a bit stressed lately. Let's try it your way."

Max reached out and punched the other man's shoulder. "There you go! I was thinking about the problem form Ben showed us. I think it's missing some things. First, it's not enough of a story." He paused letting Justin recover from the beer he snorted. "I know, I know, you think the storytelling thing is hocus, but bear with me here. Let me show you what I'm thinking."

Grabbing the other man's notebook, he quickly sketched in Justin's notebook.

When [CONTEXT], [ACTOR] wants/needs to [ACTION] but they are prevented by [BARRIER] which causes [IMPACT] that [SEVERITY]. [CONSTANTS] remain steady. However, [VARIABLES] changes [DELTA].

"See, here we start to bring together not only the context of the problem and the potential barriers but also the impact of the problem as well as the things that impact the context of the problem." He paused, letting it sink in. "Let me give you an example. Say we're talking about the geolocation idea we had last week. You remember the route-based thing?"

Justin nodded, perking up a bit. "Yeah, I remember. We were going to start work on that soon."

Max kept going, "So, if we tried to get that problem into this form, what would we have? Something like 'When going to work, a driver wants to get there quickly but can't because a recent zombie group is blocking traffic, which makes the driver late for work and gets them yelled at by their boss. The route to work is always the same. However, zombie risings happen unpredictably, as do traffic jams.' Do you see how those impacts are called out here?"

He tapped the page with the pen for emphasis. "I kept feeling like the way they were doing stories was…too little and too loose. It needed more structure, so we know if we've thought of all the things we could do. By being more thorough—more prescriptive if you will—we have a more repeatable process."

Max leaned back, passing the notebook back to his friend. He took a pull on his beer and winked. "See? We design types aren't all sticky notes and art supplies! I think we can break down our problem this way and see what we don't know."

Justin stared at the page, lips moving as he read through it.

"OK, I'm game. Let's see how we do this. Although," he said as he smiled, "are you sure we can't do one of those workshops with the art supplies? When else do I get to play with pipe cleaners?"

Max laughed. "Sounds like a personal problem to me! Let's start at the actor—the person operating the weapon."

Justin dutifully wrote down "The operator needs to" in his notebook.

"Right. So what does he need to do that he can't?"

"Kill zombies? Not get exploded by his own weapon? Have a beer?" Justin asked laughing.

"Kill lots of zombies in rapid succession." Max tapped the notebook. "Write that down."

"Okay." Justin scribbled it in.

"The context is combat. So, when trying to complete a mission."

Justin wrote it down. "Impact and severity?"

Max paused thinking, "Well, the impact is that people will die or maybe that it will take longer to kill the zombies. What would be the impact of a delay in eliminating zombies in a field situation?"

Justin shook his head. "Not sure exactly, but based on the numbers I saw today, it has to do with the cost of time in the field, risk to human life, and spread of the infection."

Max nodded. "I think this will be more effective if we can be as specific as possible, so let's put in all of those. How about constants and variables?"

Justin scratched his head with his pen. "Well, the zombies are the same. But the number and location of the zombies will vary, as well as whether they are near a populated area."

Max was pleased to see his friend was no longer talking about things like a conspiracy theorist. He nodded energetically. "OK, let's pull it all together."

After going back and forth for another 20 minutes, they had a story they liked.

"Let's show this to the team in the morning," Max said. "I think it will really help us stay focused and maybe bring up some new ideas."

Justin finished his beer and stood. "You got it. Now let's get out of here and get some sleep. It's going to be another long day tomorrow."

Key Takeaways

- Market research is a key piece to any product effort. Before investing in a product development effort, you must first determine whether there is an urgent need to solve a problem, whether that need is sufficiently ubiquitous to the market, and whether the market is willing to pay to meet the need. Marketing managers, market researchers, analysts, or product managers do this type of research prior to spooling up a development effort to ensure sufficient return on the investment. For more information on market research techniques, see *Start Your Own Business, 5th Edition* (Entrepreneur Press, 2010), and Scott Smith and Gerald Albaum's "Basic Marketing Research: Volume 1 Handbook for Research Professionals," 2012, Qualtrics Labs, Inc., http://cloudfront.qualtrics.com/q1/wp-content/uploads/2012/02/BasicMarketingResearch.pdf.

- Problem structuring methodology is a fascinating area of study that provides insight and support into how organizations or individuals can structure problems to be better able to solve them. The problem approach used here draws on research done in this area. For an overview of problem structuring methods, see J. Rosenhead's "What's the problem? An introduction to problem structuring methods," *Interfaces* 26 (6), 117–131 (1996).

Personas and Journey Maps

After being released in the morning, Sylvia and Ben started the three hour drive back into town. Sylvia yawned hugely, trying to shake herself into something that resembled being alert. She and Ben had had to spend the night at the military hospital and had been woken up repeatedly by nurses checking on them. Ben told her she was just imagining things, but Sylvia swore she heard moans that sounded like zombies several times. She knew her paranoia was likely a result of her traumatic experience coupled with her slight concussion, but she could not seem to intellectualize it and kept waking with her heart racing at every small sound.

They were told they would be allowed to interview the remaining members of the team that had handled the weapon in a day or two. One of the team members had died immediately, and another was in a coma, with severe burns and multiple fractures. The others were in bad shape but willing to talk.

Sylvia yawned again.

"Stop that! It's catching!" said Ben, yawning with her.

"I can't help it. I'm thrashed." Sylvia said. "Maybe we can talk through what we've got so we have something cogent by the time we get to the office tomorrow."

"Good idea. Although," Ben paused, "I'm not sure I can think about anything except getting a shower at this point."

© Rebecca Baker and CA 2017
R. Baker, *Agile UX Storytelling*, DOI 10.1007/978-1-4842-2997-2_10

Sylvia chuckled, "Yeah, we are pretty ripe."

Ben sighed. "You're in Uptown, right?"

Sylvia nodded.

"Perfect," Ben said. "You're less than five minutes from me. Would you mind picking me up tomorrow morning on the way in?" he gestured at his sling.

"No problem—that would be great!" she said, and meant it. She didn't like the idea of driving into the office by herself. She wondered if Ben felt the same or if it was just his broken arm.

"Now, where should we start? We need to help the team understand and consume what we've done as quickly as possible. Some of our findings are going to affect the stories they're building significantly."

Ben agreed. "Well, we need to share that the operator has little knowledge of the weapon but loads of understanding of the situation. And that the weapon isn't super-heavy, but the targeting system that we have to integrate with is." He flipped through her notes and his own, continuing to list findings that were significant.

"I think we need to start with some personas. To get some clarity on who is using this thing and how," Ben said when they finished the review.

"Hmmm…," Sylvia considered. "Honestly, can't we just do a regular report? Personas are so…fake."

"I disagree," Ben countered. "They'll be the fastest way to get the team up to speed on who we're building this for. I know they can be super-hokey when they've got, you know, like three cats and a hamster named Bubba, but that's not the kind of thing I'm talking about here," he paused, and winked at her. "Unless of course there's a hamster ownership angle I missed."

Sylvia laughed, switching lanes. "OK, I'll admit that I have a serious distaste for the goofy bits that always seems to find their way in. But also, doing real personas well takes a ton of data! I mean, we've barely got enough to generalize a bit, let alone give the details we need, like tech savviness, adaptability, and so on, with any confidence."

Ben nodded. "Fair point. However, we *do* have enough to give a rough idea of some of those things. These are really proto-personas. They're not fully fleshed out, based off the limited data we have available, but they're enough to give our stories characters that are more realistic than what we 'think' is the truth. As you know, this is a pretty specialized character we're talking about here for a very particular tool. They're not intended to be statistically representative of a population. They just need to be detailed enough to help the designers make choices. To give them some characters for the stories."

Sighing, Sylvia had to agree. "Alright, we can do personas. Or proto-personas. But with a ton of caveats about accuracy and no cats. Or names. Once a persona gets a name, it tends to take on a life of its own, and everyone forgets they are just constructs, not data made incarnate."

It was Ben's turn to laugh. "Agreed. No cats. Roles and titles only. And stick figures, no stock photos. That makes them 'just real enough' to move the story along without anyone getting attached to them."

They got to work reviewing their notes, Ben reading them aloud so Sylvia could comment. They looked for key characteristics for each role, ignoring anything about the person that wasn't relevant to the work. They were almost to Ben's apartment by the time they had sketched out three primary personas: the commander, the technician, and the squad member. As they pulled up to his security door, Ben showed them to her.

"I like them," she said. She yawned again. "Pick you up at 7 tomorrow?"

"Yep, that'll work. Go home and take a nap—and a shower!" Ben laughed and got out of the car as the security door flashed green. Sylvia watched the door shut behind him and then pulled away, heading to her own apartment. As she pulled up, she could see the walkway from the garage to the apartment was disabled again—probably another issue with the scanners. She parked in the enclosed garage and walked to the street door. Once there, she pushed her door clicker. The hum of the area scanner sounded as a blue light fanned out, scanning a perimeter of 50 yards for zombies. The door lit up green. Sylvia let out a breath she didn't know she'd been holding and quickly ran the short distance from the garage to the apartment. The bang of the heavy metal door behind her was far more comforting than it should have been.

Well after dark, feeling much better after a shower and some leftover dumplings, Sylvia leaned back looking at her laptop screen. She'd taken a nap to try to make up for the restless night, and it had helped, but now she was wide awake.

Fortunately, Ben had called with a question about one of her notes, and they had ended up talking through more of the results over the phone. One of the tricky things they would need to get across was the steps someone had to go through before and after a decision was made to initiate a zombie removal. They decided on a rough journey map to show where some of the unexpected issues arose. Sylvia had protested at first, citing that a good journey map takes time and more observations than just the one that they had. But Ben had made the point that they weren't going to have any other data coming in since the one prototype had blown up and it would be useful to help the designers identify the gaps in the experience quickly. In the end, Sylvia had agreed, and they had poured over their notes together to create the map. They chose to have the map start at the point the decision was made to engage with some zombies. The transportation issue and movement were captured as well as the need for off-site storage. Sylvia wasn't completely satisfied with it. It didn't capture the difficulties of use in a combat situation. But, a journey map wasn't the best way to deliver that information. A straightforward presentation of findings would do that. And one look at her control panel sketch would be enough to get across how maddeningly complex the system was.

After she hung up with Ben, she reviewed what they had done and made some tweaks. She had to grudgingly admit that both the personas and journey map were more consumable than the reports she usually provided. She still had reservations about their misuse, but she understood that when time was tight, it might make the difference between someone benefiting from the research that had been done and ignoring it.

It was well after midnight when she finally shut her laptop, eyes drooping. It had been an intense couple of days. She was a bit surprised at how quickly they had been able to bring the results together. But she still wasn't convinced it would be helpful.

Key Takeaways

- Personas represent a way of thinking about the user that is more "real" than looking at data in a table. Good personas are created using an aggregate of data from multiple observations of real users. Bad personas are created based on assumptions about what you think users are like. For more information on how to create personas, see Shlomo Goltz's "A Closer Look at Personas: What They Are and How They Work Parts 1 and 2," August 6, 2014, https://www.smashingmagazine.com/2014/08/a-closer-look-at-personas-part-1/ and https://www.usability.gov/how-to-and-tools/methods/personas.html.

- Proto-personas represent the first step toward creating full personas. They are useful when you have limited observations but need to move quickly. For more information on proto-personas, see Todd Elliott's "Avoiding Half-baked Personas," January 11, 2011, http://adaptivepath.org/ideas/avoiding-half-baked-personas/.

- It is important to note the difference between a persona and a segmentation. A persona is a tool—explicitly not defined by quantified characteristics—that aids in the design process. As such, they are not a rigorous research artifact and should not be treated as such. A segmentation study divides target consumers into specific groups. These studies rely on quantifiable characteristics that can be clustered, that is, grouped together statistically. For more information on segmentation studies, see Gretchen Gavett's "What You Need to Know About Segmentation," Harvard Business Review, July, 2014, https://hbr.org/2014/07/what-you-need-to-know-about-segmentation.

- Personas are important when creating stories. They provide the actor/character for the story and help keep the solution focused on the appropriate role. In addition, with sufficient data, they can provide insight into how different roles overlap, which can be key in creating efficiencies within a workflow. Personas help distance the user of the product from the reader (designer, developer, product manager, etc.), helping keep in mind the mantra that "you are not your user." Without personas, stories often default to using "the user" as the actor, which leads to confusion later as the team begins to lose focus on who, exactly, "the user" is.

- Journey maps are a graphical story tool used to convey the totality of the customer journey outside their touch points with the tool or software. Researchers use journey maps to communicate opportunities, issues, and patterns—to educate the rest of the company about the customer's experience in a way that doesn't focus on which button they clicked first. Using journey maps ensures that the team sees segments of the user's experience in their entirety. For more details on how to work with journey maps, see Megan Grocki's "How to Create a Customer Journey

Map," September 16, 2014, http://uxmastery.com/ how-to-create-a-customer-journey-map/, as well as Paul Boag's "All You Need to Know about Customer Journey Mapping," January 15, 2015, *Smashing Magazine*, https://www.smashingmagazine.com/2015/01/ all-about-customer-journey-mapping/.

Sharing the Research

The next morning, Sylvia woke abruptly, disoriented. Her head pounded, and she stumbled to the bathroom to down a couple of the pain pills they had given her at the hospital. The shower beckoned invitingly, but a quick glance at the clock told her she barely had time to get dressed and grab a juice out of the fridge. She was pulling on a sweater when her phone beeped with a text message from Ben asking if she was still able to pick him up. She grabbed her juice and her bag and made her way quickly down the stairs to the building door. Pushing the scanner, she waited for the green light. The humming continued. She started wondering what was wrong. Why was it taking so long? Her hands began sweating, and her stomach roiled as she imagined hordes of zombies closing in on her building door, scratching on the metal with their cold dead fingers. She almost screamed when the light finally turned green and the all-clear chime sounded. Taking a shaky breath, she opened the door and ran to the garage. She drove to Ben's apartment, texting him as she pulled up outside. His security door opened, and he came out, walking painfully slowly toward the car. Sylvia's eyes kept checking everywhere. Why couldn't he move faster? As he finally eased himself into the car and shut the door, she snapped.

"About time!"

Ben looked at her strangely. "Everything OK?"

© Rebecca Baker and CA 2017
R. Baker, *Agile UX Storytelling*, DOI 10.1007/978-1-4842-2997-2_11

Looking away, she nodded almost savagely, snapping at him. "Yeah, it's fine. I'm OK. Let's just get going."

He nodded, saying nothing about her churlishness as she pulled away from the curb. Sylvia tried to calm down, realizing she was being unreasonable. They rode in silence as she composed herself, one breath at a time.

Finally she muttered, "Sorry."

Without looking at her, Ben said, "OK." He paused. "Anything you want to talk about?"

She smiled sourly. "No. No, I don't think there is. Let's get to work."

They had barely walked in the door when Geoffrey rushed up to Sylvia and hugged her fiercely. She froze, not sure what to make of his unexpected affection. Stepping back, he admonished her. "No more getting blown up, ya hear? I don't have the patience for these whackos without you to run interference."

Ben walked up behind her. "Didn't realize research work was so dangerous, did you?"

Geoffrey laughed. "Yeah, well, next time how about you guys try something a little tamer? Like, you know, swimming with sharks or something."

They walked down the hall to the meeting room as they talked. Rounding the corner, they saw Max, Manisha, and Justin waiting for them. They looked tired. Sylvia tried to smile reassuringly at the group as they approached.

"So...." Max trailed off looking at her as if she might break. She rolled her eyes at him.

"Oh, please!" her bravado sounded a bit shrill, but she hoped no one noticed. "It takes more than a little explosion to stop me! Stop acting like we're breakable and get in there. We've got a lot to show you."

Max looked slightly stunned but nodded and ducked into the meeting room. Justin hesitated and then followed. Manisha stood looking at her thoughtfully a moment longer, making Sylvia squirm inside. Then she nodded her head and followed the other two into the room. Sylvia sighed in relief, cutting her eyes at Ben who nodded. The last thing she wanted right now was to relive what happened in front of her boss—she wanted to stick to the findings. She straightened her shoulders and walked in.

"Let me start by walking you all through our personas and journey map," Sylvia said as they settled into their seats. She pulled up the personas on the screen.

"Wait," Justin interrupted. "Like my personas? Buyer personas?"

"No." Ben answered. "User personas are different. They don't emphasize the things that make your customer or target customer amenable to purchasing or not purchasing your product. They emphasize those things about the user you need to consider when designing a solution. For example, whether they are comfortable with technology or are highly organized. Usually you can get general trends that describe individuals in a profession or role. They don't make up a real person, but they give you a general idea of things like how much hand-holding you'll need to provide, how to best approach the information architecture of the product, and so on. They help you empathize with the user type. Generally, we like to get a lot of data points to produce an accurate persona." He paused and winked at Sylvia who rolled her eyes again. "However, given that we have a fairly specialized set of roles that we will be dealing with and a tight timeline, we felt we could give at least a high-level idea of what type of folks will be using it and how. That said, these are not real people. Make sense?"

Justin nodded. Sylvia looked around for more interruptions and then continued.

"Our first persona is the operator," she brought up the operator on her screen. "This person is responsible for the setup and operation of the weapon. As you can see, they have excellent tactical knowledge and tech skills but may have a very minimal understanding of the weapon itself and its operation past the 'push-pull-click-click' of making it work. They will be responsible for basic field operation of the weapon, minor maintenance that may be required for setup and shutdown, and transportation details. This persona is our primary for the targeting software."

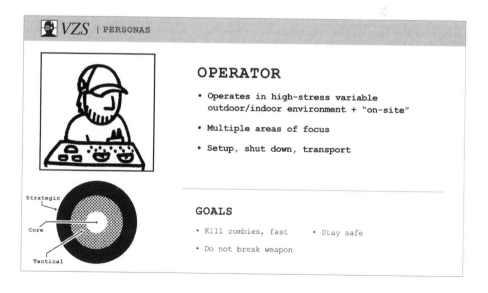

"Next we have the squad member." She flipped to the next persona. "Squad members are not primary users, but they may be expected to operate the software in emergency situations, when the operator is unable to. They will be responsible for emergency operation and setup and shutdown procedures as well as enabling transportation."

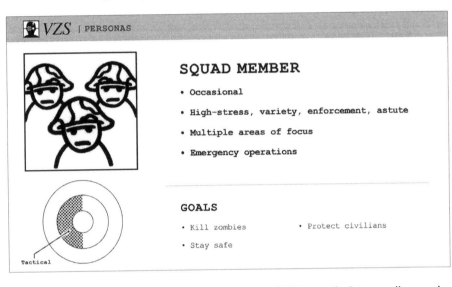

"That brings us to the commander persona." She smiled inwardly as she thought of what Sergeant Caldwell would think of her stick figure representation. "The commander has very little operational knowledge of the weapon from a hands-on perspective but has an intimate knowledge of its capabilities so that it can be deployed effectively."

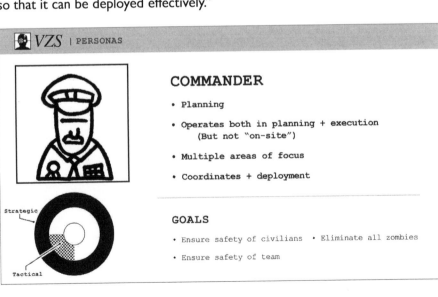

"Finally, we have the technician persona." There was a murmur as she brought up the largely blank persona sheet. She and Ben had argued quite a bit over whether to include a technician at all. But finally Ben had made the point that they wanted to ensure that the technician was represented even though they had no reliable information about the role. "You can see it's largely blank, and that is because we've heard about it and seen the need for it but haven't actually talked to anyone who does it. This is the person who is responsible for the day-to-day maintenance of the weapon when it is not in use or in transport. We're hoping to get more information on this when we talk to the inventors tomorrow."

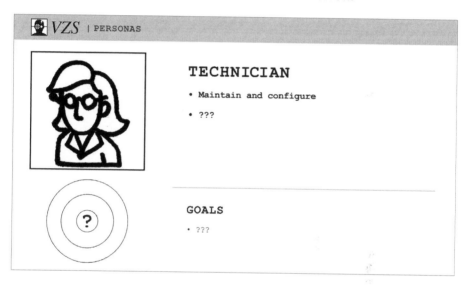

Manisha nodded. "Good. It may not impact the final approach, but then it may. Best to know where the holes are so we don't fall in."

Sylvia smiled. "Thanks. Now let's take a look at the journey map. In this map, we're showing the portion of the journey from the point at which a decision is made to engage the team and the weapon to the conclusion of the engagement."

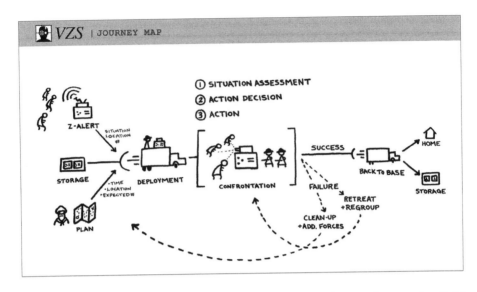

"We put this together to give more context and understanding to the field operation piece. I understand we've got some that were sketched out regarding possible weaknesses in the transportation chain?" She looked at Max for confirmation, who nodded. "Good. We can follow up with those to see if we can confirm or disprove them in our next interview with Sergeant Caldwell.

"Now for some of our observations and findings. The device itself is fairly lightweight and easily moved, but the targeting system is huge and weighty. The interface is very complicated, with multiple dials that need to be set a particular way to get things to work. This was definitely designed by someone who knew the system too well and the field work not at all. The level of complexity was...," she searched for the word.

"Stunning?" Ben posited helpfully.

"Stunning," she agreed. "Here's a sketch I made of the panel."

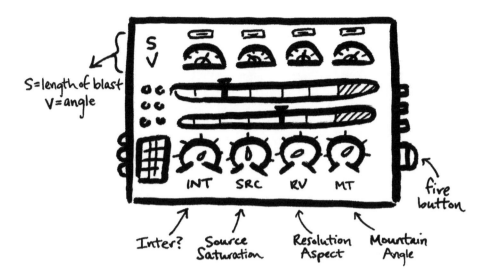

S=length of blast
V=angle

INT   SRC   RV   MT

fire button

Inter?   Source Saturation   Resolution Aspect   Mountain Angle

"The two sliders and the dial on the far right are part of the targeting system—V changes the angle, S determines the length of the blast, and the dial has to do with the mounting angle. The technician wasn't very clear how to use them and seemed to consider those controls as 'junk.' Using them moves the weapon very slowly and very poorly—it took them nearly ten minutes of fiddly setup, and they ended up physically moving the device more than relying on the targeting controls. The other three dials prepare the weapon for discharge. There's a switch that's underneath the cart you have to turn on first. The targeting technician seemed to think this was intended as a safety feature, although since the weapon only harms zombies, it's unclear who they are keeping safe. After you turn it on, it takes about two minutes to charge up. The button on the side lights up orange when it's done charging. Then you turn up the first dial until it turns yellow, the second dial until it turns green, and the third until it turns blue. When the button turns blue, you're ready to fire and can push the button. The effect seemed to be immediate—the zombie in front of it just collapsed. There was no sound, warning, or anything. Just fell over. Oh, and the dials also let you know if the machine is getting overheated—if they are all pointing to the right, you have a potential danger situation and should switch it off and let it cool down. Actually, the technician said, "and run in the other direction.""

Ben jumped in, "Discussions with the crew and observations of the operation suggest that this has only been used previously in lab settings. I don't think we can stress the awkwardness of field use enough. Any targeting system we come up with has to replace the entire system they are currently using and include considerations for weapon priming and operation—if we limit ourselves to just the targeting, it will be lipstick on a pig. We think the tech in charge of the system may know more than he realizes about it. Direct questions at the demo got a lot of blank stares, but we saw him making adjustments to the machine outside of the steps he described that suggest he has at least an innate understanding of what he needed to do to get it to work. We're hoping to talk to him as soon as possible to dig deeper."

"It's clear from our observations, the current operation does not support the need in the 'confrontation' phase. This is an obvious area of opportunity for us." Sylvia added.

The room erupted as people started talking all at once, discussing the findings.

Manisha walked over to the researchers, smiling. "Great work, guys. You two seem to be doing better than I expected, which is good, because we got clearance for an interview with the inventor tomorrow. Think you'll be up for it?"

Both researchers assured her that they would be.

Sylvia answered, "You bet! And we've got clearance to interview the team as well. Caldwell said he'd call us when they were feeling up to it."

Manisha smiled more broadly, patting the other woman gently on the shoulder. "That's some serious grit!"

Sylvia waited for the buzz to die down before she started again. "It sounds like our next step is to interview the inventors. I've got some questions we worked up last night based on some assumptions on what we need to know and the inconsistencies in the RFP, but what we really need is questions you need answered. Think about what decisions you want to inform."

She brought up another screen with close to 20 interview questions.

INTERVIEW QUESTIONS

1. Tell me about the dimensions of the weapon – height weight and so on.

2. What are some of the challenges you had creating a targeting platform?

3. What does the weapon need for optimal operation? Are there any constraints?

4. Tell me about how the weapon works from when it is turned on until it is shut down.

5. What type of maintenance needs to be performed on the weapon daily? Weekly? Monthly? Yearly?

Trevor spoke up first. "Why are these so wishy-washy? I mean, no offense." He blushed as he realized how he sounded. "What I mean is, why not ask 'How much does it weigh?' or 'Why was the targeting platform so heavy?' It seems more straightforward. Plus, don't we already have a spec telling us some of these things?"

Sylvia nodded, "I understand your thinking, but the wording is quite deliberate. It's important to keep questions in an interview open-ended. If you ask them 'How much does it weigh?' you'll get '10 pounds' or whatever is in the spec. If you ask them to describe the weight, you might get something like 'The essential pieces are 2 pounds, but the casing is iron because that's all we had to use in the shop, so it's 8 pounds, but if we had aluminum, we could totally cut that down.' The spec only says what 'is' not what 'could be.' You get much more information when you ask open-ended questions. In your second example, it's important not to sound accusatory when asking questions." She raised a meaningful eyebrow at the designer who blushed even more. "If I ask 'Why is it so heavy?' that could easily be thought of as a criticism of their design decisions. You want the interviewee to be receptive, not defensive."

Ben jumped in. "Exactly. So, let's talk—what do we need to know to make good design decisions?"

The group discussed what decisions they could make, depending on the information that came back.

"It's possible we could deviate significantly from the RFP," Manisha said thoughtfully, "especially since the only system in use is no longer usable. I'll put in some queries to find out how flexible they are. They may have to reissue the RFP anyway because of the accident."

"OK," Max said, "in that case, we need to have as much specification information on the weapon itself, without the targeting system, so we can determine if a real solution is possible. Otherwise, we're wasting our time, and we should concentrate on other opportunities."

"As much as I hate to let something like this go," Angie said, "I agree. Everything you've uncovered, coupled with the stories we have, just doesn't add up. We need to change the game if we're going to win."

After 30 minutes of discussion, the team had added another five questions around the dispersion and stability of the beam, potential environmental interferences, and hazards to operators. Sylvia wrote them down, adding them to her script.

"OK, I think we're good," she said. "It should be interesting talking to them."

Key Takeaways

- When asking for insights, stakeholders (designers, product managers, and so on) need to bring decisions to the table that research can inform. Without this level of direction, research becomes a potentially expensive exercise that yields interesting, but useless, results. Stakeholders need to have a plan for what they will do with the data that they get.

- When receiving the results of the research, it's important to ask questions to ensure a thorough understanding of what's being presented and to promote critical thinking during the research presentation. Stakeholders are not passive consumers of research data—they are active participants. Evaluative questions are particularly important at this stage. For more information on questions, see Alison King's "Inquiring Minds Really Do Want to Know: Using Questioning to Teach Critical Thinking," *Teaching of Psychology* 22 (1995): 14.

- Good interview and survey questions can be challenging to write. It's important to create a script prior to interviewing subject-matter experts to ensure that you are getting all the information you need as well as remaining unbiased and nonconfrontational. See "Creating Good Interview and Survey Questions," Purdue Online Writing Lab, https://owl.english.purdue.edu/owl/resource/559/06/.

Architecture

After the researchers left, Max turned to the room. "I want to run you guys through the story, but with a new twist I've been working on."

Manisha leaned forward in her seat, looking intrigued. "What are you thinking?"

"I was thinking about the stories and what seemed to be missing. So I went back over some old projects I'd done previously and realized there is a certain amount of detail that I gather along the way that just wasn't coming through. Some of that is because we don't have answers to all our questions, but we're not calling out the holes explicitly enough. I think this was part of Justin's initial reaction," he said as he smiled at Justin, who nodded sheepishly.

© Rebecca Baker and CA 2017
R. Baker, *Agile UX Storytelling*, DOI 10.1007/978-1-4842-2997-2_12

He stepped up to the whiteboard and wrote the problem template he'd worked out with Justin.

WHEN [CONTEXT], [ACTOR] WANTS/NEEDS TO [ACTION] BUT THEY ARE PREVENTED BY [BARRIER] WHICH CAUSES [IMPACT] THAT [SEVERITY]. [CONSTANTS] REMAIN STEADY. HOWEVER, [VARIABLES] CHANGE [DELTA].

Then he wrote out the story they had come up with.

A DEAD SQUAD IS IN A HIGH-RISE THAT HAS BEEN RECENTLY INFECTED. THEY'RE TRYING TO CLEAR FLOOR BY FLOOR, BUT THERE ARE STILL UNINFECTED HUMANS INSIDE. ZOMBIES + HUMANS BOTH COME TOWARDS THEM, BUT FOR VERY DIFFERENT REASONS. THE POWER IN THE BUILDING WENT OUT EARLIER DUE TO AN ILL-ADVISED PANICKY DECISION ON PART OF BUILDING MANAGEMENT + ONLY EMERGENCY LIGHTING IS ON. IT'S FLICKERING + SHADOWY, AND THERE ARE SCREAMS EVERYWHERE. THE TEAM OF 5 HAS TO CLEAR ALL 50 FLOORS BEFORE THEY CAN STAND DOWN AND HAVE A WELL-DESERVED BEER.

"If you put the two together, you get something like this…"

WHEN TRYING To CLEAR ZoMBIES OUT
OF AN AREA WITH UNINFECTED HUMANS,
THE DEAD SQUAD WANTS To GET RID
OF THE ZoMBIES, BUT THEY CAN'T SHooT
BECAUSE THEY MIGHT HIT THE HUMANS,
WHICH WOULD CAUSE CIVILIAN
CASUALTIES + GENERAL PANIC.
THE SIMILARITIES OF HUMAN + ZoMBIE
PROFILES CONSISTENTLY MAKES IT ↙(oTHERS?)
DIFFICULT To DISTINGUISH TARGETS.
HOWEVER, VISIBILITY + NUMBERS OF
CIVILIANS + ZoMBIES MAY CHANGE
FROM ENCOUNTER To ENCOUNTER.
                              ↖ (oTHERS?)

He stepped back. "It's less colorful. That is, it doesn't have the straight-to-the-gut feel the original does that drives empathy. But it does let us start to see more holes. Like the multitargeting—calling out that the visibility and number of zombies might change helps us hone in on needing to switch between targets rapidly for a variable length of time. By being explicit, we start to see the constraints we're working in more clearly."

Manisha nodded slowly. "This might be an effective way to start getting more specific—for requirements gathering in particular. The original story is more a vision—something to communicate and keep us all on the same track. But this version could be the iteration we need to guide our requirements gathering. And it could really help when we need to drill down to write the user stories for our sprints." She tapped a finger on her lips thinking. "I like it. Unfortunately, I think it is as far as we can take it for now."

Trevor jumped in, "I really want to get moving on the solution. It feels like we're taking forever to get something down."

"I couldn't agree more," Max said with relieved enthusiasm. He'd been itching to start work, and all the planning and investigation felt too slow. He wanted to start doing something. "Let's review everything we have to date and start sketching."

Manisha hesitated. "I know it seems like this is taking too long, but remember, there are still lots of unanswered questions here. Right now we don't know if we'll even be working on the RFP. Depending on what the government comes back with, we might be pulling out entirely."

"True, but those other business cases—the ones for international audiences in particular—there's a lot of overlap there. We could start working on some of the basic workflow architecture, and it wouldn't be wasted time," Max said.

"I suppose," Manisha said, considering.

They pulled up the stories and research that had been done so far, as well as the business cases. After a quick discussion, Trevor suggested they group the workflows in the existing products to start working out an information architecture, assuming the reuse of the primary parts of the Where's The Zombie administrative software as the guide.

"I think we should proceed as if we can get the RFP to accept letting us do the targeting hardware as well as the software. If we can't, we'll switch gears and pursue the international business case I sent you earlier," Manisha said.

Owen, Where's The Zombie lead developer, stood up from the back of the room where he'd been quietly listening next to Ward, the Virtual Zombie development lead. "Is this where you guys break out the sticky notes? If so, call me when you're done—Ward and I have some integration pieces to work out."

Max laughed. "Yeah, OK, get out of here. But we'll need you back for a sanity check and Q&A tomorrow afternoon, OK?"

"Yeah, yeah, go have fun with your art supplies," Ward said, smiling. "We gotta do some real work."

"As much as it pains me after that comment," Trevor said, "a quick sort of the current functionality of our existing interfaces and the workflows for the new interface is probably our best starting point."

"I'll get the sticky notes!" Max said, heading to the supply closet. Soon he was back with a pack of multicolored sticky notes. Justin and Angie had left, so only he, Manisha, Trevor, and Geoffrey were left.

"OK, so Trevor and Manisha, write down each of your primary features from Virtual Zombie on the blue notes with VZ. Geoffrey, you and I will write up the ones for Where's The Zombie on the yellow ones with WTZ. We'll use the pink for any anticipated feature sets not covered by the other two."

The designers got to work. Soon the table was covered in sticky notes, blue, yellow, and a few pink.

Trevor walked up to the whiteboard wall. "Based on our stories and personas, it looks like we have three primary categories of use: Operation, Maintenance, Planning. Others?" He wrote them on the board as he spoke.

Geoffrey looked at the list thoughtfully. "Where does the setup/takedown fit in with that?"

"Configuration?" Max asked.

"Yeah, that makes sense," Geoffrey agreed. "What about help? Support?"

"We usually group that with login details outside the main navigation," Trevor said. "I'm looking for primary actions that will become part of the navigation."

Max nodded. "In that case, I think that covers it at a top level. Let's get sorting."

The team quickly put the notes on the board under each category.

"OK, good. Trevor, you want to take a first crack at grouping?" Max asked.

"You bet." Trevor stepped up to the board and started pulling related sticky notes together under each category. After some back and forth, he had three to five groupings under each category. Some of the groupings had only one note, while others had three or more.

"So this first stack under Operation has Targeting, Detection, Movement, Direction, and Focus." Trevor told them.

"Hmmm…focus is from WTZ, and it has to do with choosing the area you want to detect zombies in or get a prediction for. Is that realistic for Operation, or would that be more Configuration or Planning?" Max asked.

"Planning," Manisha said. "Operation should be 'in the field" things. That sounds like something that would get set way before then."

"Maybe…," Geoffrey considered, "but wouldn't that be something you'd want to do in the field too? I mean, they might need to change the radius of focus from 1 mile to half a mile if they're eliminating as they go, right?"

"Good point—we're looking at focus for planning and focus for field use. Let's add it in both places," Max said.

"And that grouping makes sense. Targeting seems a good title," Manisha added.

Trevor added the title and went on to the next grouping. They worked steadily through the afternoon, calling out for lunch, arguing over the placement of features, and adding or removing as they went. Manisha kept bringing up the story to refocus the user goal (eliminate multiple zombies). At the end, Max stepped back, considering the result.

"I think we've got a good start. We can start cutting and pasting existing screens and wireframing new ones tomorrow."

Trevor piped up, "Sounds good. Who's bringing the donuts?"

Manisha laughed. "You are, but I'll get the coffee. Deal?"

They all agreed. Max was relieved. It felt like things were finally moving forward. In the back of his mind, he couldn't help but feel like something was missing, that they'd forgotten something important. As the team walked toward the elevators, ready to head home, he stopped Geoffrey with a hand on this shoulder.

"What do think about today?" he asked without preamble.

Geoffrey shrugged. "Good start. We've got the start of a navigational architecture that I don't hate."

"Yeah, I just feel like we're missing something," Max muttered.

Geoffrey punched him in the shoulder "Dude, we're *always* missing something. It's the nature of the beast. Go get some sleep and you'll figure it out tomorrow." He walked away while Max stood thinking. Finally, he gave up and headed toward the elevators. Maybe Geoffrey was right, and he just needed some sleep.

The next day, the designers were back in the conference room, ready to get to work, sugar and caffeine at the ready. Manisha explained they used user stories, much like development did, for the design work. "To build them," she explained, "we work directly from the problem story to flesh out the direction and acceptance criteria. One person also writes narratives from the acceptance criteria as another person designs what we use to test the designs—essentially you're writing a script for a cognitive walk-through from the requirements rather than from the design and then checking to make sure it matches. It's similar to when developers do with pair programming, with one writing the test from the success criteria while the other codes the feature."

"So, you write your own acceptance criteria? Not product?" Max asked.

"It's a team effort—they of course have a set of acceptance criteria based on the business needs. But research often adds more practical ones as does engineering. And of course we add some too based on our knowledge of the product and the space."

They called in Owen, Ward, and Justin. Max had asked Manisha where their product manager was, and she just shrugged. "Jolene has been kind of…she's not fully engaged in this product. Right before merging with you guys, we'd been doing some adjustments in titles and responsibilities. She wasn't comfortable with where a lot of it was going and made it clear she would be looking for other opportunities. It's pretty much between her and Angie at this point, but we've been operating without her for a while now."

Max shifted uncomfortably. Manisha's explanation had been brutally straightforward, and he wasn't sure how he felt about that. Sure, they were all part of the same company, and it was information he definitely needed, but he wished that somehow it hadn't come up.

When the rest of the team arrived, they reviewed the problem stories and structure on the board. Manisha led them through the user stories definition.

"OK," she said, "the problem story is at the very top level of how we're going to break this down. We'll need to address the perspectives of all four personas identified by the research team. Let's start with the Operator persona and work from there. We can use the identified goals as a starting point." She turned and wrote on the board.

AS AN OPERATOR, I NEED TO ACCURATELY TARGET INDIVIDUAL ZOMBIES IN RAPID SUCCESSION, SO THAT I CAN KILL AS MANY ZOMBIES AS POSSIBLE IN A SHORT AMOUNT OF TIME.

"You can see we drew this directly from the problem story and goals for the persona," she said. "Now let's hit the acceptance criteria—anyone?"

Justin spoke up first. "This is a lot more formal than what we usually do—I mean, development does this kind of thing, but the designs are usually already done at that point. What makes good acceptance criteria?"

The door to the room opened, and a tall woman with short spiked black hair walked in.

"Sorry I'm late, guys!" she chirped.

"Your timing is perfect, Colleen," Manisha said, smiling broadly and handing her the whiteboard marker. "We were just starting on requirements. Guys, Colleen is our business analyst. This is her specialty."

"Awesome! I love when I come in at my favorite part." Colleen swung her laptop bag unceremoniously into a nearby chair and practically bounced to the board. "Oh, hey, and nice to you meet you?" They quickly introduced the room. It seemed that Colleen had been on a hiking retreat to help document migration numbers for elk in the Pacific Northwest. She had just gotten back last night—and had been without technology for the last two weeks.

"I read up on everything you guys have so far," she said. "Good basis, but we've got to get way more specific if we're going to run with this. Good acceptance criteria are necessary, specific, feasible, and unambiguous.[1] I'm going to need your help on these because I'm still coming up to speed on the WTZ software and the gaps."

---

[1] For more information on the business analyst role and what makes good requirement/acceptance criteria, see https://www.batimes.com/articles/the-quest-for-good-requirements.html.

She looked at the board. "OK, so let's start with the user requirements. These are the requirements from the user's perspective. If the product doesn't meet these criteria for the story outlined here, it fails." She wrote on the board:

OPERATOR:

- **I CAN ACCURATELY TARGET A SINGLE ZOMBIE WITHIN A 2-INCH TOLERANCE**

- **I CAN ACCURATELY TARGET MULTIPLE ZOMBIES IN SUCCESSION, WITHIN A 2-INCH TOLERANCE**

- **I CAN SWITCH BETWEEN TARGETS WITH LESS THAN 1 SECOND LAG**

She stepped back. "Others?"

Justin nodded. "How about being able to operate it in different visibilities, like low light or bright glare?"

Colleen nodded. "That's part of our original story but not part of the requirements or observational data, as I understand it." Angie nodded her agreement. "Really, we probably need to take it out of the vision story to keep us from getting sidetracked." She glanced at Manisha.

"You're right," Manisha sighed. "We got a bit off track with that. Consider it gone."

Ward asked, "How about hands-free operation?"

Justin jumped in. "Could be good in the future, but it's outside what we need for the RFP." He looked to Colleen for confirmation.

She nodded her agreement. "That's right. Good thought, though. I'll make a note for future release considerations along with the visual issue. Any more requirements?"

No one had anything further, so Colleen continued, "OK, in that case, let's get the nonfunctional requirements down. Nonfunctional requirements outline specifics on the tolerances of the product." She wrote on the board:

NON-FUNCTIONAL:

- ## STRONG PASSWORD PROTECTION
- ## CONTROLS BOTH FIRING + TARGETING SYSTEMS

Ward spoke up, "What's your definition of 'strong?'"

"Good question!" Colleen said. "Let's assume a minimum of eight characters, mixed uppercase and lowercase, mix of letters and numbers, and inclusion of at least one special character excluding < or >. Will that work?"

Ward nodded. "That works."

"I know there's got to be more here," Colleen said turning back to the group.

"We talked about the possibility of psychological stress as a factor for design— would that go here?" Max asked.

Colleen considered that. "It could. Design stories are a bit tricky because we need to give sufficient criteria to make them well-defined and testable, without actually dictating the solution. So, we can't say 'Put a big button that says *fire!*' on it, and we can't say 'Make it simple.' How would you determine whether something is sufficiently simple to operate under stressful situations?"

"Limit the number of decision points that are emphasized on-screen," Max said immediately. Geoffrey and Trevor nodded.

"Right, you'd want to give them only the choices they have to make immediately and a way to get to other functions. But the immediate choices would have to be the biggest," Geoffrey added. "So, we'd need to give primary visual affordance to the targeting and firing aspects and de-emphasize anything else."

Justin stared open-mouthed at the designer. "Primary visual affordance? Who are you really?"

Geoffrey laughed. "Dude, just because I'm pretty doesn't mean I don't know my stuff."

Collen wrote "limit number of emphasized decision points to target and fire" on the board.

"Oh! We need to make sure other squad members can use it, but that...well, no that's stupid...," Trevor trailed off.

"Go ahead—if it's not practical, it won't go in. But it's important to get everything out, even the wild and crazy ideas. Sometimes it helps fill holes you didn't know were there."

"Well, I was going to say to make sure that zombies can't use it. But, I mean, that's just crazy."

Max said quietly, "I don't think it is. Ben mentioned something to me about the zombie that tried to attack Sylvia. She said it looked at her. Like, really looked at her. And then there's the one I saw at my window that ran. I don't know what's going on, but making sure that nonauthorized folks—zombies or whatever—can't access it seems like a good idea."

Colleen nodded and wrote "limit access to fire functionality to authorized personnel."

"Finally," Colleen said, "let's take a look at the implementation requirements. These requirements are system-level pieces that need to be in place to meet technical or contractual stuff. We include them because sometimes they inform design decisions, but also then we can reuse the story for development rather than writing a new one. We find this helps keep things organized." She wrote on the board:

IMPLEMENTATION

- CERTIFICATION PRIOR TO REMOTE ACCESS
- DOES NOT REQUIRE CONNECTIVITY FOR OPERATION
- INTEGRATES WITH FIRING MECHANISM
- INTEGRATES WITH TARGETING MECHANISM

Owen spoke up, "We can use the existing code base, right? We don't have any restrictions written into the contract on that."

Colleen nodded. "Correct. Nothing in the requirements about that."

They worked through a dozen more stories before lunch, covering what they all agreed were the primary use cases. Owen and Ward added multiple caveats as they went through, pointing out things they could use from the current products to minimize the development time. Justin, it seemed, had memorized the business case details and was able to pull the team back when they started adding too many extraneous criteria to the stories. It was hard work but effective. As they wrapped up, Owen said, "Colleen, this was awesome. And Max, I'm going to start making you guys sit in on our story times too. This was definitely helpful."

Ward laughed. "And the donuts are nice, but let's have beer next time."

Manisha smiled. "Deal. Have you guys got your sprint set up?"

Ward nodded. "Yep, we wrote up the integration stories last night and sized them. We start work after lunch."

"Excellent!" Manisha smiled. "Let's do this!"

Max's phone rang. It was Sylvia.

"Hey!" he said as he answered, "What's up?"

"Max, good news. This weapon is actually designed to be drone-deployed!"

"No way!" he almost shouted into the phone. "But, the specs...the targeting system...."

"All garbage. It was a separate contract for a targeting system that was already close to fulfillment. They had designed for a completely different weapon type—some sort of long-range ballistic I think. When this weapon came to light and needed a targeting system, the higher-ups decided they would see if they could save some money. Plus," she dropped her voice to a conspiratorial whisper, "I understand that there may have been a certain son of a certain official that may or may not have been part of the original contract. So...."

"That's awesome news! I'll let the team know right away. Thanks so much!" Trevor, Geoffrey, and Manisha were all staring at him, curious.

"No problem, boss," Sylvia preened.

"One more thing," Max said. "Do you have time for me to get Owen on? We'll need to see what kind of hooks they've got to see if our existing drone...."

"Way ahead of you. We already got access to the inventor's original designs and hooks. Honestly, after seeing this stuff, I can't imagine why the Forzare system was even considered. It's such a huge mismatch."

"Wait, Forzare? As in Forzare Combat Systems? As in the company one floor down from us?"

"That's the one. Small world, eh?" Sylvia said something he couldn't make out. "Hey, I gotta get back; they're going to show us the films they took of the original tests they did. We'll be done too late to make it back in today but should be in tomorrow. Cool?"

"Yeah, yeah, totally cool." Max waved his hand dismissively. "This is great stuff. See ya tomorrow."

"Over and out." Sylvia hung up.

"Well?" Manisha asked as he put the phone back in his pocket.

"Well, it seems like not only are drones a possibility as the targeting hardware, they were how the weapon was originally designed."

"Yes!" Trevor jumped up and danced a small jig. Geoffrey started laughing while Manisha and Max just stared.

"Dude, you are one serious whacko!" Geoffrey said slapping his leg. "Nice dance moves."

Trevor laughed with him. "You have no idea how much easier this just got. Actually," he said, sitting back down, "you do."

Max turned to Manisha shaking his head.

"Time to start adjusting the stories. And the information architecture."

Manisha nodded. "Yes, but that won't take long. And I doubt it'll affect the work we've got so far much."

With the new detail in mind, they quickly adjusted the sticky notes on the whiteboard. Max called in Justin, Angie, Owen, and Ward to catch them up. Owen seemed relieved but wanted to know when they would get the specifications in from the inventors. Max assured him that they would be coming tomorrow. He looked at the board, thinking.

Something still bothered him—a missing piece of the puzzle or maybe too many pieces. He couldn't quite put his finger on it. As he shut down his laptop, he decided to review the stories again at home, after a quick shower and some food.

Key Takeaways

- Formalizing the problem definition can identify holes in your approach and the information you have. Having a well-defined problem at the beginning of the process is key to having a successful solution.

- Creating a solution architecture early on can provide context for the design user stories, guiding the approach and how the work can be segmented.

- Defining acceptance criteria is essential. Acceptance criteria define whether a solution works or does not and removes ambiguity from the problem.

- Integrating user experience design with agile frameworks can be challenging. One approach is to break the work into two types of sprints: foundational and functional. Foundational sprints produce work that is a prerequisite for functional sprints, such as wireframes, database optimization, visualizations, and so on. By doing this, both the design team and the development team can work in a sprint rhythm, which allows for greater predictability and requires increased rigor.

- Creating a solution before having all of the information can cause a significant amount of rework. The later in the process this happens, the more costly it is.

Problem-Solving

Early in the morning, Max found himself in the conference room again, staring at the board. The functional grouping wasn't going to work. He'd laid awake most of the night thinking about how using drones changed the use cases, and it wasn't as trivial as they had assumed. The new primary use case with a drone would be remote operation rather than field level, shifting the emphasis entirely. They would need to concentrate on what had originally been thought of as Planning first and re-adjust the story. He turned as Trevor and Manisha walked in.

"We've got to pivot," he said without preamble. "Preprogramming the drone needs to take precedence. That's the primary use in the business case we've pivoted to anyway—we just didn't make the adjustments in the story and the grouping of workflows."

Trevor looked slightly confused and annoyed at this pronouncement, but Manisha walked up beside him and looked at the board thoughtfully.

"OK," she said slowly, "walk me through the new story."

Max thought for a moment. "So, it's still the same as far as the setup goes, right? But the team doesn't need to clear all the levels of the building in person—they're going to do it remotely. Um, "he paused, "but the story doesn't change really, does it? It's more how we are seeing the story that changes."

Manisha nodded. "Yes. We assumed the primary character or actor in the story was a member of the squad, not a remotely operated weapon. It's one of the downsides of having a story that's too general. We try to stay open-ended to keep from dictating the solution, but that can lead to group assumptions. It's not such a big problem since we are all working together daily, but in a distributed team…." she trailed off, pensive. "The original story still communicates the vision, but there's a subtle albeit very important change that has

R. Baker, *Agile UX Storytelling*, DOI 10.1007/978-1-4842-2997-2_13

to be made to the narrative to make sure we're refocusing appropriately. It will trickle down to the rest of the stories as well." She pulled out her laptop and typed a few lines, deleting and rewriting. Finally she looked up at Trevor and Max.

"How about this," she said, "the first part is where we introduce the change 'When trying to clear zombies out of an area with uninfected humans, the Dead Squad wants to get rid of the zombies *remotely*. They can't use *an area effect weapon like a bomb* because they might hit the uninfected humans, which would cause civilian casualties and general panic.'"

Max and Trevor nodded. "That works." Trevor said, "It adds the need for remote operation without explicitly providing the solution."

Manisha sighed. "We jumped the gun yesterday starting the work. It happens sometimes—you get information during the process that changes the story. What is important is to make sure we don't change it for just any piece of information that comes through; it needs to be something that has a real potential impact on the solution. What we've found out doesn't invalidate everything we've done, but it makes the pieces we were concentrating on much less important. Let's rethink the grouping of the off-site piece."

Max nodded enthusiastically. "Maintenance may become a nonissue for the interface too. We were thinking about all the configurations and such that had to be done on the previous system. We lost focus of the business case—we should've kept that story in mind. But if the complex configuration of the weapon is all unnecessary...."

"It is unnecessary," Sylvia stated flatly, startling Max as she walked in the room. "Ben's taking the specifications for the hooks into the weapons system to Owen and your guy." She nodded at Manisha. "And here's a copy of the video demo they originally put together when they came up with this thing. These gals were so awesome. They practically tried to hug us when we told them why we were there. I guess they've been shut out of a lot of the process and feel like no one has been listening. And frankly, after seeing the boondoggle of a field test the other day, it's no wonder."

"Boondoggle, eh?" Geoffrey sauntered in, smiling. "I just never know what you're going to say next. Clearly, I need to get out more."

Sylvia reached out and punched him affectionately in the arm. "Help me set up this video on the conference screen, and you'll see what I'm talking about."

A few minutes later, Ben had joined them, and they were all watching a very different scenario than Ben and Sylvia had witnessed previously. Shot like an amateur video, complete with twangy electronic background music, the scene unfolded.

Two young women, so close in appearance they might have been sisters, hiked into a remote area with a drone and a small brown terrier bouncing along on a leash. They reached a large clearing, spinning around with the camera with vertigo-inducing quickness. As the focus returned to the front, the dog started straining at the leash and barking. They let it go, and it took off into the woods, with a frenzy of barking. The hikers waited, breathing heavily. After what seemed to be forever, the dog reappeared, running toward the hikers, followed by a bent, naked, slowly moving form—a zombie. The zombie entered the clearing and, sensing humans, started to shuffle toward the hikers. With a shout, the hikers launched the drone, flying it toward the approaching figure. An argument broke out in Spanish as the drone waivered in the air, dangerously close to the zombie. The camera wobbled back and forth as the camera operator attempted to instruct the remote-control operator. The dog's barks became more urgent as the zombie moved steadily closer. The woman with the remote control wrenched herself away from her companion with a curse, made a quick adjustment and hit a button. The drone spun in front of the zombie, steadied, and pulsed a single red beam of light. The zombie fell over, unmoving. The women shouted triumphantly, jumping up and down, with the dog barking happily and jumping around their feet.

Sylvia stopped the film. "You can see how much simpler the operation was intended to be. All of the configuration and positioning and everything—that had nothing to do with the weapon at all. This thing was meant to be used remotely."

Geoffrey nodded slowly, "I could see a close-range application too. I mean, if you're already a combat professional, having a nonballistic option for close-quarters operation would be ideal to prevent collateral damage. Why didn't they explore that?"

Sylvia stared open-mouthed at Geoffrey.

"What?" he said shifting uncomfortably under her gaze. "I used to be a Ranger. Chill out, girl."

Ben took over in the awkward silence. "Good question. Sylvia and I noticed the same thing and asked them about it. They had considered that type of targeting as well. However, they thought the drone application had more immediate merit since there would be the potential to send it in without risking anyone."

Manisha started typing on her laptop. "I'm going to let Angie know—this angle wasn't part of the original proposal requirements, but it's worth exploring." She finished her message and hit Send. "For now, let's focus on the drone angle. With the WTZ software, locating and targeting groups is part of our core competency, and it solves the multitarget issue."

"Our machine vision algorithms should be able to handle it. So, let's update the use cases," Max said.

They called in Colleen and worked through the morning, updating the architecture and stories. Each story had to be examined to determine whether there was an impact due to the new information about remote operation. In some of the user stories they added requirements that reflected the need for using drones or other remote operation devices, adding in the need for a visual from the "weapon perspective" to the operations. By lunch, they had some completely new stories and some slightly changed stories. Max was fascinated that the original change they made to the vision story had been relatively small, but it had trickled down throughout the story structure. He wondered if they hadn't jumped the gun days ago when they had originally put the story together, working without a full picture of the problem space. Angie popped in to the conference room, bringing kabobs, salad, and several gallons of iced tea.

"Got to keep up your strength," she quipped, bouncing lightly on the balls of her feet. She piled her plate up with pita bread, hummus, and kabobs. Manisha drew her aside, speaking quietly. Max wondered what new scheme was in the works, as he poured his iced tea.

Without another word, she swept out the door. Justin appeared as she left, dramatically sniffing the air.

"Why is it the designers always get the good food? I ask for a free lunch, and Angie tosses me candy bar and a can of soda!"

"Because she knows what we do," Geoffrey said around a mouthful of pita, "unlike *some* people."

Justin grabbed at his heart dramatically, "You wound me, sir!" Laughing, he helped himself to the food and sat down next to Max.

Max dropped his voice so only Justin could hear him, "You OK, man?" They hadn't spoken about Justin's conspiracy theories since they had shared the beer at the Hollow Tree.

Justin took a drink of his tea and smiled slightly. "Yeah, I'm good. I'm still not a fan, you know, but I took off the tin foil hat. Besides, the weird sh…stuff seems to have taken a break."

Max nodded. "True, but for how long? There's still something going on, I can't seem to figure out. But I'm starting to think it's bigger than what's happening here."

Justin considered that. "Are you sure you don't need the tinfoil hat now?"

Manisha walked over and sat down next to them. "Is this a private conversation or can I join you?"

"Of course you can join us," Justin said, a bit too loudly. "I was just asking Max what the next steps are."

Manisha raised an eyebrow and looked at Max. "So what are our next steps?"

Max cleared his throat. "Well," he started uncertainly, "we've got the workplace grouping for the remote-access software, and we've decided on a hardware design for the field operation. Both are an extension of our existing software. And we've written requirements for the user stories for those designs. Colleen is writing up the development stories based off what we have now, so next we need to divvy them up and start making wireframes."

Manisha smiled and nodded. "I think we have enough cooks in the kitchen for designing. Why don't I do the write-up of the walk-throughs from the acceptance criteria?"

Justin wrinkled his brow in confusion. "The what?"

"You know what development test scripts are, yes?"

"Of course!" Justin looked slightly taken aback.

"Good! This is similar. Except instead of running the script to test the code, we run a narrative to test the design. Cognitive walk-throughs are like mini-play scripts that provide a scene and an actor. We do a mock walk-through to see if everything plays out. Someone who is not working on the designs has to write them; otherwise, you're not really testing—you're just documenting."

"Can't you just use the story itself for that?" Max asked.

Manisha shook her head. "You'd think that, but consider the development test script. You can't just use the story to verify that everything has been coded properly. You have to actually run some data through the system using a test case. Same thing here, except instead of data running through the system, we have a user running through it. Think about it like a usability test without an external user. It's a sanity check we can do before we start scheduling users."

After lunch, the designers parsed out stories and got to work. Max charted out the targeting workflow while Manisha worked through the narratives they would use to test the designs. Trevor and Geoffrey worked together, with Trevor talking through the existing workflows for Virtual Zombie and Geoffrey putting them into the high-fidelity mock-ups. When they hit a workflow from

WTZ, they switched seats. Looking over his laptop, Max watched them work, amazed at the ease at which the two designers had slipped into a rhythm. They seemed like they had worked together for years, rather than days. He was starting to think they might actually get the prototype put together in time for the proposal.

It was late in the evening when Max pushed back from his computer. He looked with a certain amount of satisfaction at the wireframes he had put together. Geotargeting was a passion of his, and this new problem had let him pull in some of his work on the dynamic route display. It had been a long day and a half, but using his prior work had really accelerated things.

He'd taken inspiration from weather maps—specifically the video feed that many of them had that showed a compressed view of the last hour of data. With these wires, you could see the early directionality of a large zombie movement and get a sense of the "rise rate"—how quickly new zombies were coming up. That could be a real issue over graveyards or anywhere the recently dead could be found. The government had, of course, mandated that all corpses be burned. But that didn't keep people from refusing to follow the order—some for religious reasons, some for pro-zombie reasons, and some out of pure stubbornness.

Manisha looked up from her laptop at him. "Ready for a quick walk-through?"

Max nodded. "Yeah, I think I am. At least, done enough for us to check some things."

She looked over at Geoffrey and Trevor. "How about you guys? Are we ready to put this thing together yet?"

Trevor nodded. "Yeah, let's do it. What we have is nowhere near done, but I want to make sure we're on the same page before we get further."

Manisha said, "So here's what I've got:

> The operator locates a nearby zombie group. She indicates the area the drone should cover, activates the drone, and sends it on its mission. She watches the action from the drone's perspective, ready to engage manual controls if needed.

She paused. "Obviously it's just part of the whole story, but it should be enough to test what we have so far."

Max nodded. "Let me bring up what I've got first." He pulled up the conceptual wireframes he had put together.

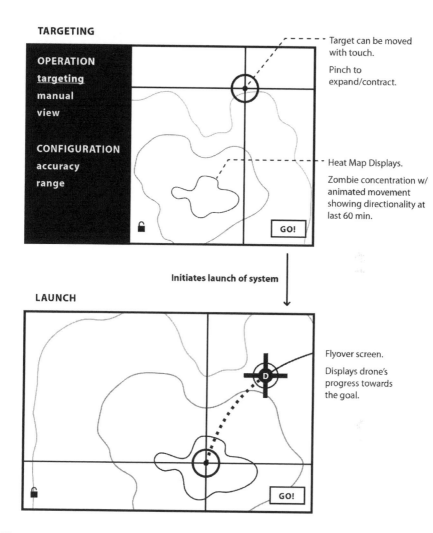

"So, the operator is going to start here with the display of the nearby area. You can see the animated heat map with the zombie movement and risings in the last hour. She would circle the area of interest with her finger and then click Go to start the drone on its way. Swipe clears the area selection, and this icon locks the screen animation to current state."

"How do we move to the drone perspective from here?" Manisha asked.

Max rubbed his face, thinking. "I was thinking she'd go through the menu, but thinking about it like this, it should flip immediately to that view."

"Good." Manisha nodded. "Anything else stick out?"

Max considered the question. "Not yet, but let's see how this matches up with Trevor and Geoffrey's designs." He stopped sharing his screen and let Trevor put up their designs. What he saw made him groan.

"Yeah, I was thinking the same thing, man," Geoffrey said with a sardonic smile. "Quite a mismatch, eh?"

The wires were so different that it was difficult to see where one would match up with the other. The basic workflow groupings were the same, but where Max had used touch patterns, Geoffrey and Trevor had opted for controls more suited for keyboard or mouse use. Not only that, but they had chosen completely different ways of providing allowances and visual emphasis. In their rush to get working, they had not nailed down many of the details needed—from the navigation choices to the input patterns—that would need to be made.

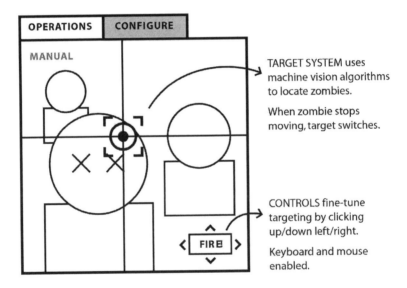

Manisha grimaced, "Well, let's pick a direction and make the changes."

Max nodded. After some discussion, they decided to go with Max's approach. It was in line with the existing WTZ software, which would have most of the reused workflows. It took a few more hours, but finally they were ready to go through the full flow.

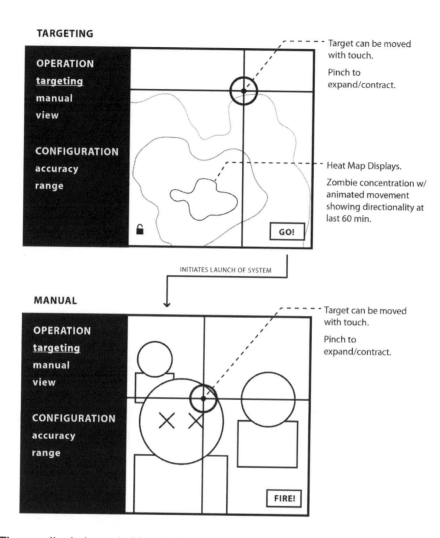

They walked through Manisha's story again. This time, both workflows fit together, and they had discussed how to move seamlessly from screen to screen.

Manisha nodded, satisfied. "OK, let's do a design review with development and product. We'll use the test story, with a few extra details, to walk them through its use. We still need to detail out the full wireframes before they can get coding, but they'll see what's coming and can raise any early flags."

Max interrupted, "Wait, why would we need to go to all that trouble? I mean, they already know the user story, so they have the acceptance criteria. Why give them a story?"

Smiling, Manisha said patiently, "Because we are presenting a piece of something bigger. Because we are the voice of the user. And because human beings like stories." She paused. "Or less dramatically, because without the story, they may focus on the wrong things, forgetting the purpose the user story fulfills. Remember, each of us has our own focus, our own perspective we bring to the table. Without stories, each of those perspectives starts to take over, warping that person's view of the design. For example, it would be simpler to implement this as a point-and-click interface rather than a touch interface. But if there is a story to remind us that this interface is intended for field use, then we realize that a mouse-driven interface won't work. Make sense?"

Max sighed. "Yeah, it makes sense." He shook his head. "Let's get this done."

Key Takeaways

- Stories provide an effective way to test your designs, in a broad sense, before bringing in users. By walking through the design using a narrative, you can identify hidden issues that may not have been obvious when you were within the design itself.

- Determining input choices, navigation, and so on, is critical to preventing mismatches. Even when working alone, it is important to document decisions of this type to ensure internal consistency within the product. For large groups working across multiple projects, style guides and pattern libraries are essential. They can prevent serious mismatches in pattern choices that can require significant rework. See Vitaly Friedman's "Taking the Pattern Library to the Next Level," *Smashing Magazine*, October 10, 2016, `https://www.smashingmagazine.com/taking-pattern-libraries-next-level/`.

- Stories help communicate how a design will be used, ensuring feedback from the design review will be helpful and targeted appropriately. Without stories, you risk your reviewers forgetting the larger objectives.

Revelations

The call came in the morning—the government was willing to change the requirements of the RFP to include targeting hardware, but not the original deadlines. They still needed to get a working prototype put together that would provide targeting for the weapon as well as an outline for their approach to the hardware. The next few days slid by in a blur. The team worked long hours, reviewing the requirements and using them to create flowcharts of workflows, sketching out the pages of the workflows at a high level, and then testing them with stories. They then took the sketches and flowcharts and created detailed wireframes that captured the interactions. Development worked around the clock to get the designs prototyped—first using the stories to work through the requirements and then using the wireframes to guide the coding. The conference room was covered in printouts of screens with markups and comments. The team returned to the stories—vision, problem, and user—over and over again to make sure they were on the right track. Max was surprised to find that having the stories made defining the requirements much easier, which made his design work go faster, providing clarity. He noticed that the common language generated by the stories made communicating designs with the development team simpler too—they already knew what he was trying to do, so the questions revolved around the specific design choices, not the intent. Even Owen, who was notoriously prickly when it came to design reviews, commented on how he felt more confident in the designs because he understood exactly how the software would be used. Early on, now smitten with the idea of using stories to move things more quickly, Angie wrote several compelling stories, outlining new use cases for infrared sensors and virtual reality headsets. But, as exciting as the stories were, it quickly became clear that they were based more on Angie's gut than any data or user requirements. Trying to drill into them to create meaningful user stories caused them to fall apart.

© Rebecca Baker and CA 2017
R. Baker, *Agile UX Storytelling*, DOI 10.1007/978-1-4842-2997-2_14

Max found himself home every night exhausted but pleased with the progress they had made. And yet something still bothered him. The explosions, the zombie in the building, the ludicrous delivery mechanism…there was something else going on. Not to mention the strange behavior he and Sylvia had both observed in zombies. He lay awake, trying to fall asleep, but his mind wouldn't let him, worrying about the problem. Finally he gave up, sitting up and flicking on a light. He took a dog-eared notebook out of his nightstand and started making notes.

Finally, his eyes started to droop. He put the notebook away and flicked off the light, drifting gratefully off to sleep.

The next morning in the office, Max walked into the conference room (Justin had started calling it the War Room) to find a woman he had never seen staring at the screens taped to the wall. Her bright floral shirt and short green business skirt seemed to brighten the room around her.

"Um, can I help you?" he said quietly.

She jumped. "Oh, sorry, I didn't hear you. I'm, uh, I'm Jolene. The product manager. For Virtual Zombie." She extended a slender hand, looking embarrassed.

Max shook her hand, studying her for a moment. Short auburn curls graced her shoulders and framed a pale freckled face. Too pale, he thought, noticing the dark circles under her hazel eyes. She looked ill, or at least overworked. He wondered why she had finally shown up after what he had gotten from Manisha.

"Can I show you around or anything?" he asked, a bit awkwardly.

"No, thanks, I got a tour of the office a few weeks ago. I'm, that is, I've been, uh, out on leave." She stopped speaking, clearly at a loss for how to continue.

"Well, I'd better get to…," Max started, when Manisha walked in, smiling.

"Jolene! It's great to see you!" Max watched as she moved forward to embrace the other woman. Jolene was clearly uncomfortable, extracting herself as quickly as she could. Manisha seemed to Max to be overly aggressive, almost strident, as she asked after the other woman's health. The tension in the room was intolerable. He started to make a quick excuse to flee when Manisha hooked her arm firmly in Jolene's.

"Let's go find Angie and leave Max to his work." She winked at him, her smile still seeming forced. "We're doing our first round of user testing today, and I know he's got some finishing touches he'll want to apply." Without another word, she hurried the protesting product manager out of the room, shutting the door behind her. Max breathed a sigh of relief.

Not five minutes later, Ben walked in with two cups of coffee, a laptop bag hung over one shoulder, and a notebook crammed under one arm. He set the coffees and notebook down on the table and started unpacking his bag.

"What's the experimental coffee of the day?" Max asked, curious. Ben apparently was quite the coffee aficionado and regularly ordered two cups—one his favorite and the other some new concoction of the barista's—every day.

"Soy milk, coconut milk, and almond milk mixed and steamed with a double shot of espresso," he said, taking a sip. He grimaced. "They hadn't come up with a name for it yet, but I'm thinking they should call it 'no thanks.'"

They both laughed. The team had grown close over the last few days of constant work. Ben continued setting up his laptop, the new coffee pushed aside.

"We've got two users scheduled today to come in for rapid iterative testing," Ben said. "The first one should be the most interesting. She fits our operator profile to a T." He paused. "The second is close but not ideal. He has the right background but is a private operator, not government. Shouldn't make a huge difference, but something we'll need to be aware of."

"Remind me again why we need a close fit for the users?" Max asked. "It seems to me we could just go park ourselves at the coffee shop and offer to buy some java for folks in exchange for a walk-through."

"Well, for one, most people won't understand the context of use—remote zombie elimination as part of a military action—outside of video games or movies. If we're going to get the tactical, fine-grained feedback, we need to make changes; we need someone who can imagine using it in real life because they've done something similar. Make sense?"

Max nodded. "Makes sense. So, when does the first test start?"

Ben checked his watch. "She's due to arrive in about an hour. Sylvia was testing the simulator when I left her."

To get testing done quickly, they had used some of their old footage of zombie risings to create a simulation experience for the "drone view" interactions. Getting it to run smoothly had been trickier than expected, and Owen had grumbled endlessly about spending more time with the simulation than the actual product. Ben and Sylvia had insisted, though, and Max felt certain that the feedback they would get at this stage could be critical. He remembered something he had written down the night before.

"Hey, Ben," he asked slowly, "do you know anything about Forzare Combat Systems?"

"The group that did that wonky targeting system? Not much. I got an earful from the inventors, but most of that was just being pissed off that no one would listen to them. I know a couple of folks who interviewed there last year. The compensation was supposedly great, but there were a lot of rumors about the company having a cash flow problem. My buddy who actually got an offer said he got cold feet and decided to turn it down."

"It seems weird they would have made something that was so completely off," Max said. "I mean, they must have done the same research we did."

"Actually, this level of research is not as usual as you would think," Ben said, turning away from his computer to look at Max. "It is often perceived as expensive time-wise, and a lot of these companies get a subject-matter expert on staff and think they don't need anything else. Total echo-chamber effect. It leads to some really bizarre products."

Max shook his head. "Even for that, it seems suspicious. Plus the sabotage…." He trailed off, looking away. He wasn't sure how to talk about what had happened to Sylvia and Ben on-site. He glanced up to see Ben grimacing.

"You're right," Ben said. "I keep trying to make it into something less… nefarious, I guess. The facts suggest that there is, at the very least, someone trying to keep the weapon from being deployed. But I'm not sure what we can do about it, other than be careful."

Max sighed. "I know. But I can't help but feel that we're missing something critical."

Ben started to answer when Justin walked in. "Hey! What's the coffee of the day?"

Ben shook his head and pushed it over to him. "Try it yourself—it's a pass for me."

Justin took a sip, grimacing. "Ugh! What's in this?"

They turned to discussing the various concoctions they had both tried. Max shook his head and turned back to the next design set from his backlog.

The results from the rapid iterative testing were interesting. The first user, a serious woman in her 30s with short blonde hair and a perpetual frown, told them in no uncertain terms that they had no idea what they were doing. The way Max had envisioned selecting the targets, while theoretically correct, did not reflect the reality of battle planning exactly. She pointed out that it was unlikely they would rely solely on the weapon, especially if civilians were involved, so there would be soldiers as well as zombies and civilians in the area. Also, most of the incursions they dealt with were in urban environments, so there would be a great deal more retargeting on the fly as the drone moved around and inside of buildings. Max listened to the recording of her critical feedback with growing chagrin. He started thinking they would need a complete redesign. As they finished the playback, Sylvia turned to the team.

"Now, I want you to keep in mind what she said, not how she said it." She said without preamble. "She approached this software with a high attention to detail, so think about the specifics of what she said and how it would affect the actual design. Most of what she's provided is very specific and actionable—and from where I'm sitting doesn't affect the approach or the design. Because we made adjustments to the story earlier, we've taken into account 90 percent of what she needs. Also, we've got another tester coming in. We'll want to get that information before we make any changes."

Max sat back and thought about it. Sylvia was right. The criticisms of the target selection, while delivered with a certain amount of disdain, were accurate and would require only small adjustments. The addition of soldiers to the targeting environment would have no impact on the design—that was just a function of the test environment.

The team was still digesting the feedback when Max realized the second user was due to arrive. He leapt up and walked quickly to the elevators to meet him. The doors dinged and opened, revealing a young man dressed in combat fatigues who walked out. Just then, Jolene rounded a corner to head to the underground. Looking momentarily startled, the young man smiled and extended his hand.

"Hey! It's good to see you, Jo!" he said, shaking her hand. "What brings you here?"

"I, um, I think you must have mistaken me for someone else," she stuttered, quickly pulling her hand out of his and walking quickly away into the elevator. The young man looked puzzled at her retreating back and then shrugged, turning back to Max who looked equally confused.

"Hey, I'm John," he said, shaking Max's hand. "I'm here to try out your software."

Max nodded, leading him to the test room. "I'm Max, one of the designers on the project. Thanks for helping us out with this!" he paused. "Do you know Jolene?"

"Jo? Yeah, I mean I thought I did. I guess maybe I did something to make her mad. She was super-friendly when I was talking to her before. We had drinks and everything. But maybe…I don't know." He looked over his shoulder at the closed elevator door. "I'm surprised to see her here. I thought she was in sales for Forzare Combat Systems."

Max started, surprised. "Really?"

John nodded. "Sure, I mean that's how I met her. She was trying to sell us some new hardware. She was good, but their stuff just wasn't up to what we needed." He smiled ruefully. "She probably just took me out to try to get the sale and is embarrassed about it now. Oh well."

They reached the user testing room. Sylvia was waiting, a big smile on her face.

"Hi!" she chirped. "I'm Sylvia, and I'll be your test administrator for today."

Max and John laughed with her, and John went in to get started.

The results from the second test confirmed what the first told them—the system needed to be tweaked for urban combat with changes to the controls to move the manual retargeting piece up in the navigation. The team regrouped, working together to make the changes. After some calls and a little help from Manisha's contacts, Ben and Sylvia found three additional testers to try the adjusted prototypes.

Ben poked his head in the room with the design team. "Hey guys, it's like 7 o'clock. You ready to roll?"

Max and Trevor both shook their heads. "No, you guys go ahead," Max said "We want to finish this part of the handoff between products, and it'll take us at least another hour."

Ben nodded his sympathy. "OK, well, see you guys in the morning. Geoffrey and Manisha, don't let these workaholics make you crazy. At least order some pizza or something."

Justin tapped Ben on the shoulder from behind. He had a stack of pizza boxes, and the smell that emanated from them was amazing. Ben popped open the top box and snagged a large slice covered in sausage and mushrooms.

"Just one for the road," he said winking at Justin. He walked back down the hall, munching the pizza happily.

Justin took the pizza in to the design team, sitting down with them.

"I wasn't sure what you guys would like, so I just kind of got a little bit of everything."

Max smiled gratefully, "Thanks, man! This is great."

Manisha nodded enthusiastically, mouth full of a slice of veggie pizza.

Suddenly, alarms blared through the office. "Alert! Alert! Zombie detected on your floor. Secure doors. Alert! Alert! This is not a drill."

Justin turned to run to the door as two shambling figures burst into the room. Trevor screamed, scrambling backward toward the wall. Manisha froze, pizza still in her hand. Justin started back slowly toward the others. Geoffrey rose from his seat slowly cutting his eyes at Max.

"Dude," he said quietly but clearly. "Tell me you brought that Glock in here with you."

"Um, yeah, I did. But it's in my bag next to the door. Behind them," Max stuttered, pointing with his chin. Geoffrey nodded.

"OK, I need you guys to grab some chairs. You're going to use them to keep the deaders away from you. Do not get bitten. Do not get scratched. Your job is to keep them away from you. I'm going to go for the gun."

At that, the zombie in the front, a formerly fat man in a rotting business suit, turned and started moving quickly toward the bag. Geoffrey cursed and jumped on the table racing down the length to get to the bag. The zombie grabbed the bag, dumping the contents on the floor. Geoffrey leapt off the table, landing next to the zombie as it grabbed the gun. He kicked at its hand, sending the gun flying. The other zombie continued to shuffle slowly toward the group at the back. Trevor was sobbing now, holding on to Manisha as she tried to simultaneously comfort him and keep a rolling office chair in front of her. Max and Justin grabbed chairs and tried to form a wall in front of her and the other designer. Just then Angie crashed through the door with a fire extinguisher, screaming like a banshee. She rushed the zombie that was trying to grab Geoffrey and bashed its head with the extinguisher. It went down in a heap. Geoffrey turned, scooped up the gun, pivoted and fired a single shot. Max watched the zombie in front of him crumple, a large hole in the back of its head. The alarm cut off mid-sentence, leaving them in deafening silence.

Geoffrey approached the zombie Angie had bashed cautiously, pistol trained at its head. Angie was panting, staring at the body. Suddenly, she threw down the fire extinguisher and sat down hard on the floor. Geoffrey poked the body with his foot. Nothing happened. Slowly, he knelt down and turned it over, keeping the gun pointed at it. The body flopped over on to its back, unresponsive.

"What's that in its ear?" Angie asked, distantly. Geoffrey frowned and gingerly rocked the head to one side. Behind the ear, something bright yellow protruded from the skull. Using a handkerchief from his pocket, Geoffrey gently pried it loose.

In the back of the room, Trevor continued to sob. Manisha was holding him now, rocking back and forth gently.

"It's OK," she whispered. "It's dead. It can't hurt you now."

"No, no, no, no, no," he sobbed. "They're going to get me. They're going to get me!"

Justin and Max looked at each other and then down at the zombie in front of them. Max shuddered. At least he'd brought the gun inside with him. But if it hadn't been for Geoffrey, it would have been useless. How had the zombie understood them? He turned to Geoffrey who was standing, bloody handkerchief in one hand and Max's Glock pointed at the ground in the other.

"What, what, was that?" he finally managed.

Wordlessly, Geoffrey held out the handkerchief. Max walked over to see what was in it, gingerly skirting the dead body on the floor.

"It's a chip," Angie said from the floor, sounding tired. "An electronic chip."

Max looked. It was as Angie had said, an electronic chip. Bright yellow on one end fading to orange on the other, covered with a bit of gore, it lay in the middle of the clean white handkerchief, another mystery.

"Why would it have a chip in its head?" Max asked. Geoffrey shrugged, wrapping it carefully up in the handkerchief. He quickly checked the Glock, engaged the safety, and flipped it handle first to give to Max. Max accepted weapon nervously, rechecked the safety, and set it on the table.

"I don't know how it got a chip in its head or why," Geoffrey said, "but I know that it didn't put it there itself. And I know that it understood us and moved in a way it shouldn't have been able to." He shook his head. "I've never seen anything like that, in any of the encounters I've had."

Max wondered how many times Geoffrey had been in combat. When he'd hired the easy-going designer, he knew he'd served five years in the Army Rangers, but he didn't know much more than that. Today, he felt like he had a glimpse of the man's past.

"I think I know what's going on," Manisha's voice wavered slightly from the back of the room. She stood, extracting herself from Trevor and looked directly at Max. "It's not good."

Key Takeaways

- Stories can accelerate the process of software delivery by improving requirements definition and the level of detail and vision that is communicated to all team members. By providing a common language, the story keeps everyone focused on the same goal. However, while stories can invite a greater level of detail and rigor, they can also obscure the details and provide confidence where none is merited by burying the lack of information in emotional language and rhetoric. To avoid these pitfalls, ensure that stories are based on data about real problems. Good stories stand up to rigorous examination and questioning. Bad stories will fall apart.

- Stories used throughout the process can be used to create test scripts for use with users, which ensures consistency in intent. See Sarah Gibbons' "UX Stories Communicate Designs," Nielsen Norman Group, January 15, 2017, https://www.nngroup.com/articles/ux-stories/.

- Getting research at an early stage prevents the echo-chamber effect, in which people with similar opinions or ideas reinforce each other, without being open to or aware of key facts outside their experience.

- Rapid iterative testing is a way to gather targeted feedback on specific areas of the product and then make changes to the product based on that feedback to retest. This type of testing is particularly useful when needing to refine a product prior to entering full development in a short time frame. See Michael Medlock et al.'s "Using the RITE method to improve products: A definition and a case study." (2002). Presented at the Usability Professionals Association 2002, Orlando, Florida.

- Taking the information from user tests to iterate on design immediately can help improve the product cheaply—before costly coding investments have been made.

MVP

"I've been trying to put the pieces together for weeks," Manisha said. "The demo explosion, the zombie in the office, the mismatch of the targeting system with the weapons capabilities—it all was so strange."

She sat down in a chair, looking suddenly tired. "I kept trying to figure out why a company would essentially sabotage their own project. It made no sense. Until this." She gestured at the chip. "It's Forzare. It has to be. They've developed an implantable control for zombies. It turns them into weapons. With something like this, they can create zombie soldiers—disposable and effective. They won't stop, they can't feel pain, and they pose the added risk of infection. If the weapon we're working with was effective, it would severely impact their effectiveness. They must have pulled in some favors to develop the targeting hardware and then sabotaged it to make it look like it was useless. They probably planned on offering the weaponized zombies as soon as they had them perfected."

"But," Justin protested, "that's illegal. Zombie experimentation for purposes other than finding a cure has been strictly forbidden. It's unethical."

Manisha nodded, glumly. "I know. But that doesn't mean people aren't doing it." She sighed. "When Trevor and I worked together at StillHuman, we tried to help people deal with the fact that their loved ones had become zombies and to protect their rights. So many companies out there—more than you would think—try to prey on those who contain their loved ones in hope for a cure. The approach them with a lot of long contracts and a promise that they are looking to restore them. But in reality…," she trailed off looking sadly at the body on the floor. She took a deep breath and continued, "In reality, they are experimenting on them to turn them into weapons or mules or worse."

"Mules?" Justin asked softly.

© Rebecca Baker and CA 2017
R. Baker, *Agile UX Storytelling*, DOI 10.1007/978-1-4842-2997-2_15

"Drug carriers." Trevor answered in a clipped voice. "If you can get a zombie to pass for human, you can implant anything you want in its body. As much as you can fit. We saw one case where—"

"Trevor," Manisha interrupted him with a look. He stopped, "I'm sorry," she said. "It's not a...happy story."

"I bet." Angie said, still seated on the floor. Max thought he'd never seen her still that long. She looked up at Geoffrey with a slight smile. "What next? Who do we call? I don't have a number for this in my contact list."

"I've got this one," Manisha said, sounding weary. "We need to call the authorities. They'll want to know about the chip and the deliberate negligence with the targeting system." She pulled out her phone and started making calls.

"What I don't get," Justin said, "was how they got the zombies in here to start with. I mean I know we're in the same building and all, but how would they get access to the floor? There's an access code after 6 p.m."

"Wait, Angie, does Jolene have the access code?" Max asked.

Angie looked surprised. "Well, yeah, of course she does. She hasn't officially decided to leave yet, and I didn't see a reason not to let her have access to the office. I mean, we're hoping she stays. She's a pretty sharp cookie, even if she has some reservations about the position."

"Reservations?" Justin asked.

"You know, the usual concerns about money and advancement. Nothing out of the ordinary. She wanted a more senior title and a bump in pay and thought she could get it with the merger. But we're not in a place to give a raise until we win the contract, and you know how I am about title inflation. Wait, why did you want to know if she had access?" she asked, swiveling on Max.

"Because I might have an idea about how they got access." He outlined his conversation with John, the second tester. As he talked, he could see the realization hit Angie. Her face clouded with anger. By the time he finished, he wouldn't have been surprised if steam was coming out of her ears.

"When I see her," she sputtered, "I will throttle, no, I will fire, no I will, *argh*!" She smacked the ground with her hand and stood up, starting to pace. "I don't know what I'm going to do, but she is going to be sorry she ever messed with me!"

Manisha looked up from her phone. "They're on the way. We need to meet them at the elevator."

Max looked around the room. Trevor was huddled in a chair, clearly trying to pull himself together. Manisha looked exhausted, dark circles under her eyes, staring off into nothing. Angie was pacing angrily back and forth muttering about what she would do with Jolene once she got a hold of the woman. Geoffrey was leaned casually against the wall, watching Angie with a slightly amused, if detached, smile on his face. He turned and saw Justin looking at him.

"You and me, bro," Justin said winking. Max shrugged, and the two of them headed out to meet the cavalry.

The investigation seemed to take forever. There were questions and more questions and then more questions. Max was certain he had answered the same question from the same three questioners at least twenty times. Manisha had said it was to help confirm the facts since eyewitness accounts were so unreliable. Max was starting to think it was simply to torture him. He was tired and hungry—the pizza had gone cold, and no one had the stomach for it after the attack—and he just wanted to go home. A squad of people in biohazard suits came and took away the bodies after cataloging them and taking a million pictures. They also took the chip. Geoffrey answered even more questions than Max but seemed completely unperturbed talking with investigators as if they were casual acquaintances who had run into one another at the coffee shop. They took and bagged Max's Glock and the fire extinguisher. Finally, well after midnight, they were allowed to go, after being instructed that they were not to come back for at least 24 hours. Angie protested but only weakly—even her ever-present reserve of energy was exhausted. Max stumbled out to his car and headed home, wondering what the next day would bring.

The week after seemed to fly by in a blur. When the team returned to the office two days later, all traces of the incident had been removed. The building had even replaced the conference room carpet. Trevor was unable to come back to work and took a leave of absence while he tried to recover. When the next round of user tests confirmed the validity of their refined approach, Geoffrey and Max worked furiously on the new iterations, barely staying ahead of Owen, Ward, and the rest of the development team.

Finally, it was time to present the prototype to the committee. They decided Manisha should do the honors. Max, Ward, and Angie hovered in the back of the room while Manisha stepped up to the front. Owen and Geoffrey waited at a coffee shop down the hallway. Manisha smiled broadly and brought up her first slide.

VZS PERSONA

MEET JENNIFER

She's a member of a deader squad, dedicated to downtown Dallas.

She's been asked to go in with her squad and eliminate 30 or more zombies from a high rise. The only problem is that the building is full of innocent people. And the power is out.

She and her team need to get in and get out quickly and make sure there are no civilian casualties. She's anxious but determined to do what needs to be done.

OBJECTIVE:

+ Kill 30+ zombies
+ Ensure team and civilian safety

CHALLENGES:

+ HIGH-RISE
+ POWER OUTAGE

"Meet Jennifer. She's a member of a deader squad, dedicated to downtown Dallas. She's been asked to go in, with her squad, and eliminate 30 or more zombies from a high-rise. The only problem is that the building is full of innocent people. And the power is out. She and her team need to get in and get out quickly and make sure there are no civilian casualties. She's anxious but determined to do what needs to be done."

Several committee members leaned forward, already interested.

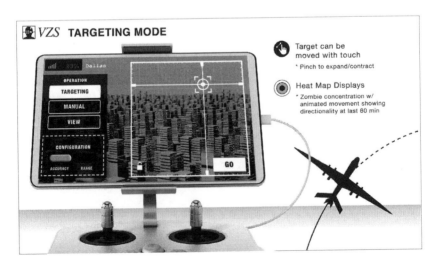

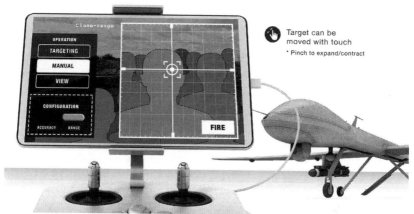

"Today, we're going to show you how Jennifer can use the Virtual Zombie Systems solution to locate zombies by their movement signature and eliminate them with a close-quarters drone, quickly adjusting to situations on the fly. Rather than talk, I'd like to show you a short video of what Jennifer's mission would look like." She looked at the lead committee member, a short woman with gray, close-cropped hair. She nodded briefly, and Manisha started the video.

An hour later, the team walked out of the committee review, stretching. Angie was grinning ear to ear.

"Did you hear those questions?" she asked excitedly as they walked to the coffee shop. "They're already acting like they own it. That one guy actually started asking how soon it could be combat ready!"

Manisha nodded, looking pleased. "They clearly related to the story and its use. I think we nailed it."

Max was shaking his head in slight disbelief. Even after everything he'd seen so far, he was amazed at how readily the committee had aligned with their presentation. He overheard two of the members talking, saying how it was a relief to get a group in that really understood who would be using the weapon and how.

"Stories are powerful. But, what if it's the wrong story?" he asked quietly. Manisha turned and looked at him sharply.

"That's the thing, isn't it?" she said after looking at him for a long moment. "Our brains...they love a good story, almost to the exclusion of everything else. It's great when you can use them like we did today, to show the solution to a problem. But," she paused, looking back over her shoulder at the committee room, "it can also be misused. How simple would it have been to go with a different scenario—maybe one that supported our open-air operation. If we hadn't adjusted our story and design to fit the facts that we uncovered, we could have told a different story. And our audience might have believed it. It's incumbent on us to ensure that our stories are as close to the truth as we can get."

Max nodded slowly. No matter how powerful or compelling the technique, there were no free rides.

Key Takeaways

- Using stories to communicate your design to stakeholders helps them step outside of their perspective and empathize with the users. See Whitney Quesenbery and Kevin Brooks's *Storytelling for User Experience: Crafting Stories for Better Design* (Rosenfeld Media, 2010).

- The same story can and should be used throughout the process. Depending on the intent, more or less details can be included, but the primary story should remain the same, changing only if data is introduced to suggest some part of the story is inaccurate. By keeping the same story throughout the process, the team remains focused on the same outcome as originally scoped. Changing the story at various points introduces opportunities for miscommunication and feature creep.

- Stories can be misused. They make what we hear easier to understand and remember. But they can also lead us astray by misrepresenting the facts. Good, ethical stories require due diligence and data. See Jonathan Gottschall's *Theranos and the Dark Side of Storytelling,* Harvard Business Review, October 18, 2016, https://hbr.org/2016/10/theranos-and-the-dark-side-of-storytelling.

The Bid

One week later, Max found himself stuck in traffic again. He shifted into park and switched channels on his radio, bored with his usual podcasts, when suddenly something caught his ear.

> In tech news today, the FBI announced that the Dallas-based software company Forzare Combat Systems is under investigation for contract fraud and exploitation of zombies. They have made several arrests, including CEO Larry Copeland. Forzare Combat Systems was unavailable for comment.

Max smiled. He had lain awake more than once in the last few weeks wondering if the government would actually take action. Sometimes things worked out. His phone rang, startling him. He flicked on the speaker phone, turning the radio off.

"What's the password?" he said.

"We got it!" Angie squealed. Max winced at her volume.

"That's great, Angie," he said, craning his neck to see if the traffic in front of him was breaking up any time soon.

"Well, try to be a little bit more excited about it, would you? I mean it's only our freakin' paychecks here!"

"Angie, I'm excited, I promise. It's just…well, I'm stuck in traffic."

"Don't be a baby," she said, "do some deep breathing or whatever. Look, we've got a ton of work to do when you get in. They loved the idea of the close-quarters application. It's more hardware intensive, but they want us to handle it. Oh! And the inventors are coming into the office tomorrow. They're going

© Rebecca Baker and CA 2017
R. Baker, *Agile UX Storytelling*, DOI 10.1007/978-1-4842-2997-2_16

to be working directly over the next year to get this thing live. So get out of that traffic and get in here! No time to waste. Plus, I brought donuts."

The line went dead. Max shook his head. Same old Angie. He wondered whether there would be any donuts left by the time he finally got out of this traffic jam. Flipping the radio back on, he cranked the volume as an old Metallica tune, "Sandman," came on. Singing along, he tapped a rhythm on the steering wheel. Deep breathing, he thought derisively, whatever.

Just then, he saw a shambling figure moving toward his car. Great, he thought, another deader. As it got closer, his breath caught and his hands gripped the steering wheel with white-knuckled shock. The once-bright floral shirt was dirty and ragged now, the auburn curls in disarray, and green skirt dull even in the sunshine. It turned and looked at him, and he swallowed, heart racing. It was Jolene. She grinned and moved slowly but deliberately toward his car, keeping eye contact. He tried backing further into his seat. Sirens sounded. Her head swiveled in the direction of the noise and then back to Max. She cocked her head, as if listening to something he could not hear. Then she grinned wider, winked at him, and ran off the side of the road. Max stared after her, breathing hard. She quickly disappeared into the brush. He couldn't see where she'd gone. A deader cruiser slipped slowly by, looking for the zombie they would not find. He wondered what they would say if he told them where she went…and that she winked at him.

A loud honk made him jump. Traffic had started moving again. He put the car back in gear and started driving, wondering what was going on.

The team was gathered in the war room with donuts and coffee, as Max told them about sighting Jolene.

"But I thought," Sylvia said, glaring at Max, "that Forzare got shut down!"

Max held his hands up, one clutching a donut with pink sprinkles, in mock surrender. "I know! I thought so too! I'm just telling you want I saw."

Ben rubbed his jaw, thinking. "Well, we don't know for sure that Forzare made the chips. Or that Jolene was working for them."

"Right!" Geoffrey chimed in while reaching for a habanero-mango iced donut. "They were clearly involved, but they may not have been the only ones. Did that guy, John, ever tell you which company Jolene was selling hardware for?"

Max thought, chewing thoughtfully. "No, I don't think he did. But I gave his information to those agents that we talked to, so I'm sure they followed up with him."

Angie shrugged, talking around a powdered-sugar donut. "I don't care. She's out of our hair now. End of story."

The others looked at her in horror. Angie looked around puzzled, "What?"

Max shook his head, "Angie, that was kind of harsh even for you."

Angie sighed looking down, "OK, look. You're right, that was harsh. I'm still mad at her. She betrayed us, you know? I spent so much time with her, trying to get her to understand why what we're doing is, you know, amazing and important. And she just stabbed us in the back. But you're right. I'm sorry."

Manisha reached over and gave her a quick hug around the shoulders.

"Yeah, yeah, all good, you know?" Angie muttered.

"So, tell us about the new project already!" Geoffrey said. "I mean, I'm good with the donuts, but you said we've got additional work."

"Right!" Angie said, standing up quickly and dusting her hands off. "Next steps. We need to get on this new targeting piece. We included a suggestion in our bid to expand the scope to include hand-to-hand combat targeting in addition to the drone targeting. We'll need to do some discovery to nail down the requirements, but I think we've got the right people to get this done.

She turned to Manisha grinning. "What's our story?"

Key Takeaways

- Story closures can take many forms—they can be deliberately open-ended as with a problem story, or they include a prescribed result as with user stories. It is important to understand why you are telling the story and what you want the audience to take away from it.

- Data is at the heart of any good software development effort and, as such, at the heart of any good story. Stories without data move from useful tools to simple entertainment.

Epilogue: Finding a Happily Ever After

This has been a story of stories. By traveling along with Max, Sylvia, and the rest of the team, you have seen how stories can be used to enhance communication, keep people on the same page, bring the stakes faced by your users to life, and persuade others. You have also seen how they can lead you astray or send you down the wrong path if you are not careful.

Problems

Problems are the key to a good story and a good product. Problems are also hard. Oftentimes companies jump straight to the solution stage, which is totally understandable—solutions are fun, and it feels good to create them. Puzzles are popular for a reason! But jumping straight to the solution leads to

© Rebecca Baker and CA 2017
R. Baker, *Agile UX Storytelling*, DOI 10.1007/978-1-4842-2997-2_17

having a solution in search of a problem, which is not a good (or profitable) place to be. Problems are hard because defining problems requires a lot of up-front work, and at the end, you still don't have a solution. To define a problem well, you need the following:

- *Accurate and sufficient data*: In the story, the first problem definition the team tried to come up with failed because they didn't have accurate data (in their case, that the weapon was designed to be mobile). Once they had better data, they were able to create a successful solution.

- *Context*: Context lets you understand the circumstances surrounding the problem. The team originally understood the context of the problem (urban zombie removal) but gradually let that context change into something else. It wasn't until they got more data in the form of user tests that they recognized their mistake.

- *Actors*: You must understand who the players are in your problem space and how they interact both with the problem and with each other. Understanding the overlap (or lack thereof) for multiple roles ensures a complete understanding of the situation and hence the problem.

- *Desired result*: Before you can figure out what the problem is, you must first make sure there is, actually, a problem. For this, you need to identify your desired result. What do you or your user hope to accomplish?

- *Barriers*: Once you know your desired result, you can look for what stands between you and that result, or your barriers. Barriers come in many forms—they could be a process that adds three days to a release cycle, a lack of equipment or expertise, or a door that is too short—but they all keep the actor from accomplishing the desired result. Barriers are the heart of the problem, and overcoming them will identify the solution.

- *Constants and variables*: Knowing what changes and what doesn't helps focus on the factors that will help you solve the problem.

Stories

Stories come in many flavors, but they build off the problem. Stories lead to or even describe a solution and can be used at all levels of the process. These are some of the types of stories I covered:

- *User stories*: These stories are the ones most familiar from Agile. They include the success criteria and are often used to estimate work. They follow this canonical form: "As a USER, I want to ACTION, so that I can GOAL."

- *Job stories*: Job stories are an evolution of the user stories that include context: "When CONTEXT, as a USER, I want to ACTION so that I can GOAL."

- *Problem stories*: Fully detailed problem stories explain the circumstances of the problem without suggesting a solution. The following is a form you can use for this: "When CONTEXT, ACTOR wants/needs to ACTION, but they are prevented by BARRIER, which causes IMPACT that SEVERITY. CONSTANTS remain steady. However, VARIABLES change DELTA."

- *Horror stories*: These are stories that let you explore the problems that could arise. One possible form for these is as follows: "EVENT plus CIRCUMSTANCE = RESULT (negative)." The key to writing horror stories is that you are looking for a way to circumvent or prevent the negative result.

- *Test stories*: These are stories that walk through how you expect the user to interact with the product. Test stories must include all of the acceptance criteria from the user stories as part of the narrative.

Journey mapping, which the team briefly explores when looking for sabotage opportunities, is a type of graphical storytelling. Usually used to show a sequence in time, journey maps consist of Before, During, and After events. Within each of these categories, they show how actors and context and events interact. Journey maps are particularly useful when multiple paths are possible and you want to identify opportunities or potential problems.

Characters

Characters are what bring your story to life. They are the users of your product that you must build empathy with. They are the antagonists your users must overcome. They are the customers who will buy your product.

Characters are initially based on assumptions but must be verified with data to be truly useful. In this story, Ben uses *explicit* and *implicit* characters to identify research opportunities and then identifies how much is known about each one to determine what type of research needs to be done. These characters are merely roles based on the current understanding of how the product will be used. They are deliberately sketchy because the team understands they will need to be adjusted later.

After some initial field observations, Ben and Sylvia decide to use proto-personas to communicate some of their findings. Proto-personas and personas are a good way to help people understand your observations. However, both should always be based on data and observations, rather than your imaginings of what your users are like. If you have never met with and observed a user, you should not create personas. How detailed the persona is—whether you use stock images, give them a name, and so on—depends on the amount of data you have to create them. If you have lots of observational and secondary data, it helps to create a more detailed persona because it is likely more accurate. Less data should result in less detailed personas, with cartoonish faces and no personal details.

A quick word of warning about characters and personas—much like your favorite hero or heroine in a novel, characters and personas can start to take on a life of their own. As long as that remains within the context of the story, it can add depth and color to your narrative. However, once the character steps outside your story and starts "helping" you create new stories, you tread on dangerous ground. Characters and personas are not real. They are based on an aggregate of data that provides a reasonable facsimile of a human that does a thing. But they are created very specifically to do a particular thing. Because they are so appealing and relatable, many teams find themselves swept up into considering those characters' wants, needs, and motivations for parts of the software they were never intended to touch. Be alert to this tendency and keep your characters and personas locked up safely in their narratives.

The Importance of Data

As you may have noticed, data is the unsung hero throughout this story. When data is ignored or missing, bad things happen. When data is plentiful and included, success follows.

Unfortunately, much like defining problems, gathering and interpreting data is hard and time-consuming. This leads many teams to "go with their gut" or "wing it." This, in turn, leads to a number of problems such as these:

- *Cognitive biases*[1]: Cognitive biases are how our brain "fills in the blanks" when faced with insufficient or incomprehensible data. Confirmation bias (only looking for data that confirms your current beliefs), sunk-cost bias (continuing to invest in a failing product in an attempt to recover the previous investment), and anchoring (focusing on the first experience as representative) are only a few of the cognitive biases that can lead to poor decisions and costly mistakes.

- *Solving the wrong problem*: Without data to inform the problem creation, teams often choose what they perceive as the problem. As most software development firms do not produce software for other software development firms, this leads to solving problems as seen by software developers—not the end users of the product.

- *Missed opportunities*: Without data, you don't know what you don't know. Most environments are rich in opportunity for solutions, but you must enter that environment and observe it in order to be able to identify where you can provide a solution.

Integrating Design with Agile

Integrating design work in Agile can be done in a number of ways. Lean UX, Agile UX,[2] and design sprints[3] all approach the problem differently with varying levels of success. One method that can be effective in enterprise software is a design-infused approach.

The following process outlines the expected activities and deliverables at each stage of a design-infused Agile process.

---

[1]Wilke A. and Mata R. (2012.) Cognitive Bias. In: V.S. Ramachandran (ed.). *The Encyclopedia of Human Behavior*, vol. 1, pp. 531–535. Academic Press.
[2]Marcin Treder, "Lean UX vs Agile UX—Is There a Difference?" https://www.uxpin.com/studio/blog/lean-ux-vs-agile-ux-is-there-a-difference/
[3]Jake Knapp, *Sprint: How to Solve Big Problems and Test New Ideas in Just Five Days* (Simon and Schuster, 2016).

Discovery and Planning

During discovery and planning, the team explores the market opportunities and pain points of their end users. Research and analysis happens during this phase, gathering sufficient information to ensure that things go smoothly once development begins. The idea funnel starts very wide at this stage, and mistakes are cheap to correct. Sufficient time must be spent in this phase to avoid expensive mistakes and badly timed or targeted releases. Investing in this phase ensures quality and efficiency. This phase can be broken down into the following stages:

- Discovery and ideation
- Product solution definition
- Business opportunity assessment
- Vision and validation
- Scope and acceptance

Discovery and Ideation

During this stage, product management investigates the current business landscape, assessing the potential opportunities and risks in the marketplace, interviewing customers, and understanding the competitors. The output of this investigation is business cases, also known as *problem definitions*.

DISCOVERY

Product Solution Definition

Business cases provide the perspective of the market and the customer. Product solutions should solve the problems stated in the business cases but should take the perspective of the user—frequently a different person from the customer with different motivations in enterprise software. To create effective product solutions, product designers, working closely with technical leads and product manager, should own the solution definition, ensuring that it is technically feasible and will solve for the stated business problem.

Business Opportunity Assessment

Once the product and business research has been completed, product management, design, and development can collaboratively evaluate the opportunities and provide significant detail to enable an accurate scoring of the business opportunities available.

Vision and Validation

During this stage, the detailed design directions are solidified and vetted. Primary workflows and architecture should be defined, technical approaches should be solidified, and success criteria should be determined at the epic level; there are also potential measurement opportunities during this stage. Approaches are play-tested with customers,[4] and effort estimations are done at the epic level.

Scope and Acceptance

During this stage, detailed stories are written, estimated, and groomed for the backlog. The backlog is prioritized, acceptance criteria are finalized, and release dates are determined. Potential dependencies and risks are identified. It is important to note that stories are created for *all* team members—design and development.

For a design-infused Agile sprint cycle, design and development work together in two types of sprints: foundational and functional.

- Foundational sprints create items necessary for the functional sprints such as wireframes and visual comps, back-end services, APIs, and so on.

- Functional sprints use items from the foundational sprints to create an MVP.

- Functional sprints cannot start until at least one foundational sprint has been run.

- All team members may participate in foundational sprints.

---

[4]Jon lay and Zsolt Kocsmarszky, "A Lean Approach to Product Valication," *Smashing Magazine*, July 5, 2016, https://www.smashingmagazine.com/2016/07/a-lean-approach-to-product-validation/.

Foundational and Functional Sprints

During the foundational sprint, dependency items are created—wireframes, visual comps, prototypes, back-end services, tech debt, and so on. This type of sprint enables the regular functional sprint. Foundational sprints include sprint reviews, planning, and estimation just like traditional Agile sprints.

Functional sprints are simply traditional Agile sprints,[5] with the expected outputs and functions.

Happily Ever After

Making software is fun but challenging. You can spend months creating a perfect solution. However, if you haven't defined your problem, understood your story, and verified it all with data, chances are that your perfect solution will be nothing more than beautiful, useless, electronic art. The world is filled with interesting problems, waiting for someone to take the time to notice them, tell their story, and give the characters a happily ever after.

---

[5]Understanding Agile Methodology, http://agilemethodology.org/

Get the eBook for only $5!

Why limit yourself?

With most of our titles available in both PDF and ePUB format, you can access your content wherever and however you wish—on your PC, phone, tablet, or reader.

Since you've purchased this print book, we are happy to offer you the eBook for just $5.

To learn more, go to http://www.apress.com/companion or contact support@apress.com.

Apress®

Printed in Great Britain
by Amazon